Advu

How does one become acquainted with one's inner strength and manifest wholeness? Reading Barbara Stahura's personal essays is both a delight and an answer to that question: By paying attention—to dreams, thoughts, the words of others, and the details of one's surroundings. Embarking on a spiritual journey helps, too, when it is in conjunction with living deeply, as Barbara does, both in her love, her self-reflection, and in the very real fear of losing her beloved to injuries sustained in an accident. Life is difficult and wonderful, and Barbara helps us find our feelings and rejoice.

> — Sheila Bender, author of *Writing and Publishing Personal Essays*

Certainly the topics Barbara Stahura covers in these essays are diverse, unique, and entertaining, but it is her crystal clear, crisp, intimate writing style—her ability to enable the reader to engage and embrace both the topics and the writer herself—that is the real strong suit of this book. Even Kerouac and Thoreau keep the reader at arm's length while intimately sharing their views on the world, but Barb throws her arms wide open, welcoming the reader to relish not only her world and the people in it, but her very spirit as well. Bravo, Barb."

> — Harvey Stanbrough, National Book Award nominee

With wit and insight, clarity and compassion, Barbara Stahura explores love, loss, and transformation in *What I Thought I Knew*, a collection of personal essays. Listening only to her heart, Stahura answered the sacred call to a writer's life. These inspirational essays document her subsequent journey toward self-sufficiency, understanding, spirituality, and self-healing.

> — Susan Cummins Miller, author of the Frankie MacFarlane Mysteries

At the heart of these linked essays is the story of a love that blossoms in midlife, only to be tested immediately by a nearly fatal motorcycle accident, a love that proves to be the most powerful force in healing both the author and her injured husband. This recent history confirms Barbara Stahura's intuition, built up over years of reading and reflection, that our experience of love is the nearest we come to sensing the energy manifest in the myriad forms of this flowing universe. Her insights into what she calls the "holy mysteries" are hard won and movingly told.

> — Scott Russell Sanders, author of *A Private History of Awe*

"Whether it's serving God or writing essays, building boats or raising children, every call arises from passion," writes Barbara Stahura. And passionate about writing she is. Whether she's describing her husband's near-fatal motorcycle accident and recovery from a brain injury, or her bare-ankled encounter with a rattlesnake, her words rise off the page. Her heartfelt memoir, full of humor and insight, depicts a life charged with uncertainties and fears, bravery and joy, a life showing what it's like to be a writer and more, what it's like to be human. *What I Thought I Knew* is an engaging and transformative read.

> — Ken Lamberton, author of *Time of Grace: Thoughts on Nature, Family, and the Politics of Crime and Punishment*

What I Thought I Knew

What I Thought I Knew

Barbara Stahura

Dear Linda,
Even in China, always
remember: changing your
mind can change
your life.

Barbara Stahura
8-30-08

Wyatt-MacKenzie Publishing, Inc.
DEADWOOD, OREGON

ISBN 978-1-932279-99-3

Library of Congress Control Number: 2008929179

Portions of the Introduction are taken from the essay "Dreams of Going," published in *Writing and Publishing Personal Essays* (Silver Threads, 2005) by Sheila Bender

"My Dad and the Sphinx" appeared, in an earlier version, in the online edition of *Science & Spirit.*

"Following the Call" appeared, in an earlier version, in *Science of Mind* magazine, February 2001.

"Overcoming the Wobblies, Or Those are the Brakes," appeared, in an earlier version, in *Sculptural Pursuits*, Spring 2006.

"Fallow Time" appeared, in an earlier version, on MoonDance.org.

Sections of "Riptide," from *Science & Spirit*, Jan./Feb. 2005, have been used in "Brain Wreck."

Excerpt from "Invocation" is used with permission of Teresa Roy.

Excerpt from "The Truelove" from *The House of Belonging* by David Whyte. © 1997, printed with permission from Many Rivers Press, Langley, Wash. www.davidwhyte.com

Cover Photography by Wendy Sizer.

Contact the Author: www.BarbaraStahura.com, barbara@barbarastahura.com

Wyatt-MacKenzie Publishing, Inc.
DEADWOOD, OREGON

www.WyMacPublishing.com (541) 964-3314

Requests for permission or further information should be addressed to:
Wyatt-MacKenzie Publishing, 15115 Highway 36, Deadwood, Oregon 97430

Dedicated to Patricia Stahura

The most important things I know about my mom have never changed. She has always been the one unwavering, loving constant in my life, for which I am extremely blessed.

Acknowledgements

I send my deepest thanks to Dee Schneidman, who, without knowing their profound effect, uttered the words that literally changed my life and became the inspiration for this book: "Maybe it's time to give up what you think you know."

My dear friend and colleague Bob Yehling nudged me to write a book of personal essays. When I was finally convinced, he offered fruitful suggestions that helped me overcome my reticence and fears. This book would not exist without his encouragement. Thank you, Bob.

Many thanks to the Wednesday Writers—Penny Porter, Valarie James, Marcia Rorke, Lesley Lupo, and Sally Scott—for their willingness to slog through various drafts of many of these essays and offer pertinent, lively comments in person.

Thanks also to my long-distance writing buds, Marilyn Noble and Becky Allen, for the same encouragement, only via email and phone. And to Teresa Roy and Caroline Nellis in Indiana, and Susan DeBow in Ohio, all magnificent women and inventive writers who have long been an inspiration and a support, many thanks.

I couldn't have completed this project without my editor, Nancy Linnon, and her invaluable guidance and reassurances that both the book and I would be fine.

I can't forget Goldie, our black cat, who came to sit on my desk around 4:00 every afternoon and insisted with gentle pats to my face that I get up from my chair to stretch—well, really, to feed him dinner. I am part of his staff, after all.

And to my husband, Ken Willingham, who insisted that I take the time to follow my heart and write this book, and who wouldn't let me doubt myself: Thank you, Sweetheart. I am your Boo forever.

Introduction

When I was a little girl in Hammond, Indiana, I would often lie awake on summer mornings and listen for the whistles of distant trains. The cool, dewy air carried their music through the open window next to my bed. I was still far too young to join them in their travels across the country, but they inspired me nonetheless. Perhaps someday, I, too, could travel to another city and become someone new: a confident girl who was neither painfully shy nor too smart, who was not the ugly duckling belonging nowhere, nor the one who tried too hard to be good and who read about life instead of going out to meet it, because inside a book she was safe.

Blossoming from that shy, lonely girl, I became a woman who is much more confident and outgoing, with only a lingering shyness. I have ridden trains, in truth and in imagination, to become the person I am. I am still smart, and glad of it. I still do my best to be a good person, but not out of fear and not because parents and nuns tell me to—although the lessons they provided made me conscious of the importance of goodness in the world. I still feel safe within the pages of a book, but I also feel sure of myself out in the world.

Sometimes, I wake up early in my grown-up bed, windows open around it, and hear the distant whistles of trains. It is then I remember that little girl who did not yet know the most important thing her grown-up self would learn: Life is all about choices. Learning how to change your mind, when the moment is right, is often the best gift you can give yourself.

TABLE OF CONTENTS

CHAPTER ONE
My Dad and the Sphinx

The photograph isn't what jolted me; it was too tiny and blurry to make out the details of the five men on horseback. The pang of recognition sprang from the familiar handwriting looping across the back. "These were taken in front of the Sphinx," my father had written. "I'm 4th from the right. Old Moe (the guide) rode a donkey on this tour. By the way Moe has 3 wives and I don't remember the no. of kids."

I turned over the World War II photo and squinted at the indistinct face of this young soldier, identified by the shape and tilt of his head. This man, later to be my father, had traveled to Egypt and stood before the Sphinx! To see him in such an exotic locale stunned me.

When my father died of lung cancer in 1966, I was a week shy of eighth-grade graduation. Because we were not a family to sit and reminisce, my knowledge of Daddy's life outside our small circle was limited. He was just my dad. Of course, I knew he'd been in the war, grown up in McAdoo, Pennsylvania, where he picked huckleberries, and enjoyed liver and onions. The little I knew about him was an observable kind of knowledge, like knowing that a book will fall if you push it off the table or that certain plants can't bear fruit without bees to pollinate them. None of it revealed the essence of who he was, what he meant his life to be, or how he coped with tragedies, such as the deaths of his youngest son or his hero, President Kennedy.

I feel silly admitting something so obvious: Not until I was in my early 40s and pulled this photo from a box of jumbled family pictures during a visit home to Mom's, did I see my father as a full-blown person with a singular history of his own. At the same instant, this bit of paper announced, as had nothing before, that my father was lost to me, along with any deep, real knowledge of him beyond the few superficial details I had managed to glean.

Thomas Edward Stahura was a sergeant in the Army Air Force and a radio operator on a B-17 bomber stationed in Foggia, Italy. That's how he got to Egypt: he and his buddies had flown there, as part of a mission or perhaps on leave. In a series of photos, he smiles his toothy smile, his service cap covers his black hair, and his crisp uniform hangs smartly on his slender frame. He is very young and surrounded by the camaraderie of his buddies, whose names are also recorded on the backs of the photos taken in Egypt, Camp Tel-Litwinsky in Palestine, Jerusalem, and Bethlehem. On the back of another of the photos, he'd scrawled, "It was a swell trip." The terror of flying under anti-aircraft attack while dropping bombs on cities and enemy emplacements is not apparent here.

Only a few years later, he began his life as the husband and father in a middle class, Catholic family in Hammond, Indiana. The son of an alcoholic coal miner, he rarely drank, although I'm told he had a shot of whiskey to celebrate the birth of his first child: me. He labored in factories, taught Mom to drive, painted the house, mowed the lawn, sat at his desk in the bedroom to pay bills and write letters, and owned one suit, a serviceable brown one. In 1952 he built our house on Maplewood Avenue with help from his brothers Paul, Max, John, and Leonard, who pitched in again a dozen years later to finish remodeling the basement after the cancer had weakened him. Sometimes we kids asked what he was doing, even though it was obvious he was cutting the grass or painting the siding on the house, and he teased us with a straight face: "Shoveling snow." A religious man, he never cursed; when angered or frustrated, he cried, "Darn it to heck!" He was a strict father, but in the early years he still laughed with us, the corners of his blue eyes crinkling.

When our family traveled by train to Seattle in the summer before I entered first grade, I snuggled on his lap in the observation car late one night as the train pulled into a station somewhere out West. We were nearly alone in the car, domed by windows, as the train chugged from the empty, black night into the glare of lights and the bustle of travelers. I remember his love surrounding me but not a word of what we said. When we arrived back home after our vacation, a letter from our parish, St. John Bosco, was waiting to reveal whether or not I'd been accepted into the first grade at their parochial school. Daddy and I were standing by the front door, the breeze from the elms along the curb flowing in through the screen as he knelt down on one knee so I could sit on the other. He read the letter to me—I had been accepted—and he was pleased I would have a Catholic education.

"You're a smart girl," he said, "and you'll be a good student there."

It made me happy to know he was proud of me, and I always worked hard to be a good student and a good girl.

Later, when I was far too old—10? 11?—he spanked me. I have only the blurriest recollection of my minor infraction—sassing Mom perhaps—but he would not tolerate it. He sat on a chair in the laundry room, which was in the basement. Who remembers, all these decades later, if he used his hand or the wooden paddle that normally hung near the refrigerator, with the words "Board of Education" painted on it in cheery colors? During our few minutes there, sunlight filtered into the subterranean space through the ground-level window, and it sparkled on the backyard grass above our heads.

I cried more from anger and humiliation than the slight sting. Spankings were for babies! How could my father do this to me when I was so grown up? He sent me to my room, and despite my shame, the only thing I could think to do was try to make things better with him again. He needed to know I was still a good girl and wouldn't do bad things anymore. What would I do if my dad didn't love me?

I walked down the hallway to his bedroom and hovered in the doorway, sniffing back tears as he worked at his desk. He knew how much I loved him. Certainly he would smile and open his arms to pull me in for a big hug. I would be forgiven, and all would be well between us.

"I'm sorry, Daddy."

He didn't even look up from his papers: "Don't do it again." No salve, no salvation, in his voice.

My dad had always comforted me. When I was little and couldn't sleep, I'd go into the living room when he was watching TV late at night, the voices turned to a low hum, and he would pat the couch and beckon me up next to him. But today I had done something he thought terrible enough to deserve a spanking, and now he wouldn't even look at me. Something tore in my chest—I could literally feel it—as my heart twisted and broke, severing for me something elemental in our relationship.

Now I can see how he simply could have been distracted with paying bills, or how he might have been embarrassed about the spanking and couldn't own up to it. Probably he didn't realize my fear or the intensity of my need to repair things between us. Anything in the world could have been on his mind—had he known about the cancer yet?—but back then I was only a little girl who believed her father had rejected her. Years later, after I'd gone away to college, a TV commercial showed a sad little girl in long braids shyly approaching her father in his easy chair. He smiled, lifted her into his lap, and held her. I sobbed the first time I saw it, and my husband, unnerved by the flood, cradled me in his arms.

In my early teenage years, Daddy became distant and even more strict, often unreasonably so, Mom told him. I had always been a good girl, and I still was. Why couldn't I watch the Beatles on TV or listen to rock-and-roll on WLS out of Chicago? We both struggled to control my life, and I pulled even farther away. I did my best to avoid him and quashed any impulse to take my problems to him. He wouldn't understand. Besides, he had already turned his back on me.... Better to stay away.

Daddy's appearance in those wartime photographs is happy-go-lucky, even jaunty. He later grew tormented, suffering bouts of moodiness and depression. He often railed against "Big Corporations" that treated the "Little Man" unfairly and kept a cache of file cards with notes for a book he was going to write on the subject. He even walked off the job at the Mobil Oil refinery in East Chicago where he worked at the time to protest what he believed was a dangerous condition. Even though co-workers agreed with him (management, of course, did not), they stayed put when he walked out. He was unemployed for seven months.

His religious beliefs also added to his inner turmoil. Always devout, in his mid-30s he gradually turned even more fiercely to religion. He joined several Catholic service organizations and spent innumerable hours helping poor people in our parish, some of whom took grievous advantage of him. By the early

1960s, these "good works" he was so determined to do took him away from us. "When will Daddy stay home?" we asked Mom, who was angry at his neglect. Even Daddy's priest friends—kindly Franciscans named Hermes and Eugene—could not convince him that God did not mean for him to sacrifice his family for strangers.

When I was in my late 20s, Mom revealed to me how Daddy had matter-of-factly informed her that he would be dead in two years. It was the spring of 1964, and she was pregnant with their youngest daughter, Jennifer. For some reason, I envision him delivering this message to her in the kitchen, perhaps as she prepares dinner, with the sunlight from the window over the sink illuminating them both. She hears these crazy words, looks at her husband—only 40 and apparently in fine health—and scoffs. Of course, she doesn't believe him. Does she think, *boy, he's really gone around the bend now?* Does she look at the calendar and mark the date in her mind? Does her heart contract just a little, just for a second, wondering if he could be right? It was bad enough he was already away from home so much; would he next leave her a young widow with five children to raise?

The next year, he developed a cough that would not go away and was diagnosed with lung cancer. (Never a smoker, he had worked in filthy factories and oil refineries.) He indeed died two years after their conversation, to the day: He had written the date on a file card and stashed it in his desk, where Mom found it after the funeral.

On that day—May 26, 1966—I was only 14 and did not know of my father's premonition. He was gaunt with the cancer by then, wasting away and hardly able to breathe. My parents' bedroom, with an added hospital bed, often smelled weirdly salty because of the frequent night sweats that tormented him and also kept Mom awake all hours changing bedclothes and sponging him clean. A small gate across the doorway prevented Jennifer, then a toddler, from wandering in and swallowing the pills on his bedside table, which also held a small bell he rang when he needed something; his voice was growing weak. If we got too rowdy and noisy, as five kids are wont to do, he pounded on the wooden floor next to his bed with a broomstick. Down in the basement where we spent a lot of time, the pounding rang along the rafters like thunder.

Of course I could see all this. I couldn't escape it; no one in the house could. But I had no close experience of death, except for my youngest brother, Michael, who had died a few days after birth and whom I had never even seen. Unlike today when dire illnesses are freely discussed, back in the 1960s, cancer was "The Big C," and it was spoken of only in whispers; children were not included in the discussion. Given the times, it was likely we kids were never told that Daddy's illness would eventually kill him. But he had broken my heart long before this, and by now, I was a teenager and self-absorbed. The Beatles, secret crushes on boys, and books occupied far more of my attention than my father's illness did.

Before May 26, Daddy had been rushed several times to St. Catherine's Hospital, and always he had been treated and sent home. But on that day, soon after I came home from school, he began gasping for breath and the ambulance arrived again. He had always come home before, so I didn't worry much. I did my homework and took advantage of his absence to turn up the volume on my radio. But several hours later, Mom came home and told us our father had died. He was 42 years and three days old.

One night soon after his funeral, I woke up, spooked by the feeling of strange happenings in the house. I went to Mom's bedroom, where the hospital bed and salty odor were gone. She was awake, too.

"Mom, I'm a little scared. Something weird is going on."

"I feel it, too. And I saw something in the kitchen"—which she could see from her bedroom door—"like black smoke floating in the air. But I'm not scared. I think it's Daddy coming back to make sure we're okay."

"Really? Can I sleep with you?" I was 14.

"Sure."

Over the years, on visits home to see Mom, we would often rummage through the box of family photos she kept on a shelf in her closet. In one black-and-white photo from Spring 1952, Mom holds me in her arms. She is wearing a plaid skirt and white blouse. I'm only a few months old, chubby and bonneted. Daddy is to our right, a proud husband and first-time father mugging for the camera. He's wearing light-colored trousers and a dark jacket and tie; his feet are deliberately planted slightly apart in the grass. He holds his chin high and his back very straight, his left arm behind Mom and me. His right arm is cocked at the elbow as he holds his fedora by the brim and rests it on his forearm. In another photo taken around this same time, I'm seated in a high chair, big-eyed and bald and edging toward a giggle as I watch Daddy, who's kneeling before the chair in profile to the camera and grinning broadly at me. In a photo from our train trip to Seattle in 1956, our family at the time—Mom, Dad, Jean, Marty, and me—stands on Mt. Rainier, laughing at being able to make snowballs in July.

By April 1965, we had changed. A photo from that time must have been taken after church: Daddy is wearing his brown suit and I'm in a dress and Sunday shoes. A few cousins and siblings crowd below us on the front porch, but on a higher step Daddy and I stand stiffly a few feet apart. I look sad; he seems stern. Yet, since this is only thirteen months before his death, perhaps his diagnosis—of which I was then unaware—already weighs on his mind. In any case, our separation is evident, and whenever in later years I looked at this frozen snippet of family history, I felt sad all over again. He had only a little more than a year left, and in that time our relationship would never thaw.

Even before he predicted his death, Daddy was praying for it. Mom revealed this at the same time she told me about his premonition. Once while cleaning their bedroom, she came across a letter he left lying open on his desk, still unfinished. Addressed to his friend Fr. Hermes, the letter was Daddy's plea that God send him throat cancer, although he gave no reason for this bizarre request. All those years later, Mom and I wondered if Daddy had been haunted by his service in the war, or if perhaps his torment was due somehow to a father who may have been abusive, a secret once heard through the family grapevine. And why specifically throat cancer? Did he want to be silenced for some reason?

We never solved the mystery. But now, since I have no time-line on which to place the spanking and the letter, I wonder if they somehow coincided. Did he write the letter around that same time? Was he by then contemplating death?

This tormented man, who seemingly both feared and desired retribution for a sin for which he could not atone, was my father, and I didn't know him at all. We didn't grow older together, and he left no messages for me, in his looping script or otherwise. We never talked about Egypt, or how it felt to know he was going to die so young, or what I hoped my life would become. Left stranded in the time warp his early death forged in my broken heart, I was the defiant and confused little girl he never got to see grow up, while he remained the one-dimensional man whose early death left him silent and secretive as the Sphinx.

Beyond the summer of 1966 came high school, college, marriage, and a move to California. With each big change in my life, I wondered how my father would have felt. Would he have understood when I gave up religion and searched for spirituality through paths that were less dogmatic? Would he have approved of my husband? Would he have beamed with pride over my degree from Purdue University? Would he have missed me when I moved across the country, or been sad when I divorced? Or would he have continued to grow more distant and guarded, still obsessed by his "good works"? If he had lived, would we ever have healed the wound between us?

With no answers available, my desire to solve the puzzle of my father's love became mostly forgotten, like a once-cherished piece of jewelry broken in some way and then stored in the back of the drawer. Once in a while, though, the golden glint would catch my eye again.

I was living in Southern Indiana, in Evansville, on the day in 1993 when I turned 42 years and four days old, older than my father ever was. In the years since his death, I often had sensed his presence, although nothing like Mom's black smoke had ever appeared. It was more a familiar sensation enveloping me, like protective arms on a train in the dark Western night. I think the first time it happened, I was in my late 20s and living alone in Sacramento after my divorce. Washing the dishes one evening, I turned away from the sink to wipe tomato sauce spatters off the stove, a wet dishcloth in my hand. And there it was—pleasant, warm, and friendly. It was so unexpected, I stopped in mid-wipe. It faded after a minute or two.

Hmmm, I thought. That was nice.

It happened again from time to time, while I was reading,

taking a walk, eating dinner or doing something else, but always when I was alone. I couldn't ignore it. At first, I liked pretending it was Daddy letting me know he was nearby because I now felt protected and loved; that was as far as I could go. Then one day it appeared and I said aloud, "Hi, Daddy," and smiled because saying those words felt long overdue and good. No one answered, but the feeling lingered and grew a little stronger before it faded. Yes, I decided, it was him. After that I always greeted him and sometimes added, "Thanks."

Sometimes I wondered: why couldn't he have made me feel this way at least one more time before he died?

In 1994, my women's writing group was on retreat at a small center in Kentucky, across the Ohio River from Evansville. On Saturday evening, Laura was talking when her head began to hurt. The sharp pain in the middle of her forehead made her sit down, unable to continue. Then she stretched supine on the floor, hands to her head. Several members of the group gathered around her, trying to help. As the pain grew worse, Caroline asked for an ice pack, which she applied to the base of Laura's skull. Other women applied Reiki and used various methods to comfort Laura.

I sat nearby on the couch, with no skill to add to Laura's care, but I had an idea. In recent years, I had suffered debilitating headaches myself, which I eventually discovered to be stress-induced: I was tightening up the muscles in my head and neck so much, they became like a tourniquet, constricting blood flow to my head and causing pseudo-migraines. Once I learned to keep those muscles relaxed, the headaches disappeared.

So I leaned forward, hoping only to make things better, and said to the group on the floor, "If she tried to relax the muscles in her head and neck, maybe that would help."

Caroline, one of my closest friends, looked at me.

"That won't work," she snapped, and turned back to Laura. "This is serious."

My breath caught as an ancient emotional link flung me back in time to that day in my father's doorway.

She didn't mean to be unkind, said my rational self. She's just worried about Laura.

But simultaneously I felt that old tearing in my chest, and my broken heart keened with the pain.

Quietly, I sat back in the couch, tightening my throat against tears suddenly welling up. No one noticed. I was glad. How embarrassing to be falling apart when Laura was in real distress.

I left the small conference building to cross the yard to my room. While the others stayed with Laura, I broke open in the dark, rural Kentucky night. Tears began to fall as soon as I was sure no one would see. Then sobs rolled up, rising from where I had so carefully stitched together my old father wound, now sliced wide again by a chance remark that somehow struck the same aching place that wanted only love. Curled in bed, I cried until my eyes were swollen nearly shut.

It was not the only time I'd felt this pain after that day with Daddy. Other times, remarks made by others wrenched some stitches in the wound. But this night, the blast came full force.

See? said my battered heart. *The damage he did was permanent. You'll never be over it.*

By the time my roomies came to bed after Laura had been taken to the hospital (she had suffered a brain hemorrhage but would fully recover, thanks in part to Caroline's ice packs slowing the blood flow), I had fallen into an exhausted sleep, as desolate over my father as I had ever been.

Daddy had been dead more than thirty years by the time I attended an Integral Journal workshop at Mt. St. Joseph Retreat Center. There was certainly no chance to learn much more about him now; time had stretched too far and memories had waned. Besides, the protective feeling appeared every now and then. That was enough.

For one exercise during this workshop, our instructor, Joe Zarantonello, asked us to sit quietly with our eyes closed while visualizing a bridge over which a teacher would walk towards us. Then we would write about the experience.

I'd done many exercises of this kind at various workshops and in my own meditations. No matter who or what appeared, the results were always intriguing. At another women's writing retreat, we were instructed to meditate and allow a protector to appear. Perhaps, suggested the woman leading the meditation, it would be a powerful female figure, like a she-bear. But mine was most definitely male, an eight-foot-tall angel named Josiah, with shoulder-length blond hair, a sword, and widespread white wings—rather hunky, in fact. Another time, a proud warrior woman named Estella came to me, with her wild, wiry, salt-and-pepper hair and a purple cloak that fell to her ankles. A third guide, a young girl I named Golden Child for her abundant yellow tresses, never spoke, as Josiah and Estella did, but communicated simply by thought. Whatever these guides were, they had all helped me understand myself better.

I eagerly expected the same kind of being to appear at this retreat.

I settled back into my chair, feet flat on the floor and hands in my lap. Almost as soon as I closed my eyes, a most improbable bridge appeared in my mind. Crossing a small creek in a meadow, it was painted white and made of wood, yet it was a smooth half-circle, which would have made it impossible to walk over had it been real. However, I didn't question its shape; I simply asked my teacher to appear. As I stood at one end of the bridge, the top of a head covered with thin black hair appeared on the other side beyond the crest. As my teacher continued to mount the bridge and come toward me, more and more of his face was revealed. It was Daddy. He looked joyful and robust, not gaunt and pain-wracked as I had last seen him. He was smiling his familiar toothy smile, his blue eyes crinkled at the corners—those eyes!

During my daily meditations over the previous few weeks, I'd seen a pair of gentle blue eyes looking back at me as they floated in my mind. I didn't know to whom they belonged, only that they offered me great comfort when they appeared. My father had been announcing this visit.

Daddy arrived at my end of the bridge and enfolded me in a hug so perfect and single-minded it smoothed away all the pain I'd ever felt with him. This was my *real* father, the one I remembered from my early childhood. I was now older than he had ever been in life, yet I was still his little girl; we hadn't spoken in thirty years, yet he knew everything about me and was proud of the woman I had become. No words passed between us, yet I somehow *knew* all these things.

As all of the half-dozen workshop participants did this exercise, layers of hard, physical reality surrounded us, like nested Russian dolls: the retreat center grounds, the conference building, the room in which we sat, the tables before us and the plastic chairs beneath us, and finally the limits of our own skins. Yet, when we closed our eyes and opened our minds to all possibility, time and space did not exist; whatever universe we tapped into or created there for ourselves was boundless and perfect. It was from this luminous place that my long-dead father spoke to me.

We continued holding hands as we broke from our hug and stood apart, gazing at each other. He was beaming like the young man in that early photo who was so proud of his little family, yet an old, peaceful wisdom flowed from him. I was nearly floating with happiness—my dad had come to see me! Starving for so long to know everything about him, I now understood there was only one thing I needed to hear.

"I love you, Barbara," Daddy said, his eyes soft with love. "I never stopped loving you, even though you thought I had. There was so much to do, so much I *had* to do, in that life, and my time was so short. Something had to move aside to make room, and I'm sorry it was you and the other kids and Mom. I'm so sorry, Sweetheart."

He pulled me close once more. In my vision, I stood and held him tightly, while in physical reality I sat unmoving in my chair, afraid to break the spell. If he had lived, I thought, it would have been like this.

"Yes, it would have," he said aloud to my unspoken words.

With that, he faded and my universe gently compressed again. I was back in the conference room, stunned with joy, tears streaming down my face.

My father has been dead forty-two years, and still I have no answers to the many questions about his life. In that regard, he will always be as silent and secretive as the Sphinx. And since the day of my vision, more than a decade ago, the protective feeling has never returned, nor has my father appeared in a vision or any dream I can recall. But neither has the pain in my heart, even in situations in which it once would have wrenched me apart. Intellectually, I can never know for sure what happened during the meditation at Joe's retreat, but that doesn't matter. My heart knows the truth: my father's spirit came to visit for those few numinous minutes and surrounded me with the same love and comfort he had wrapped around his tiny daughter that night on the train. Daddy never stopped loving me, and that's all I needed to know.

CHAPTER TWO
Following the Call

Call, calling.
From crayon box to uncapped pen,
From history known and yet to know.
This is the call rousing you from sleepwalk,
Rattling bars of your dreaming dungeon soul;
This is the call that is calling,
Come, come home.

—Teresa Roy, "Invocation"

As a girl going to Catholic school in the 1950s and 1960s, I had two passions, although using that particular word then would never have occurred to me. The first and most enduring of these two things—reading—was my greatest pleasure as well as my safest place. As soon as those black marks strung across the pages of books began to dance themselves into words for me, the world opened, and I became an eager, voracious reader. Reading almost anything was fun. Like the entire *Golden Book Encyclopedia*, "Aardvark to Army" through "Wales to Zoos," that Mom brought home volume by volume from Burger's grocery store, where they were sold for only a dollar-something apiece. How else except by reading would I have learned that, while taking a bath, Archimedes discovered how some things sink and others float? How else would I have learned that towels soak up water by something called capillary action, or that the aurochs was an ancient kind of cow from which today's cows are descended?

My stacks of library books took me to exotic places far beyond Northwest Indiana. I traveled to the Egypt of the pharaohs, or long-ago America when the thick forest could swallow up a tiny pioneer girl. I journeyed to wherever Nancy Drew or the Hardy Boys were solving another mystery. When I was swaddled in the pages of a book, my pal Mike didn't drop my hand as though he had accidentally touched a dead animal and announce to all the Red Rover players that it was too sweaty to hold. My stomach didn't get all scared when I thought about trying to ride my bike, enveloped by that horrible wobbly feeling that yanked me to the ground almost every time. My ears didn't hear the chatter at recess about the last slumber party I hadn't been invited to. I didn't have to worry that the boys on whom I had secret, desperate crushes would find out and be mortified, which would have humiliated me, the terminally shy, brainy girl of the class.

My second and mostly secret passion: I longed to be a nun. Life in the convent at St. John Bosco surely would be peaceful and protected; the other nuns wouldn't mind my shyness. They were smart and liked books, too, so I would fit right in. I would devote myself to prayer and good works while living with kind, strong women as we supported one another in our calling to the same high purpose. Best of all, I imagined how we friends would exist in happy community while joyfully working together for God and His son, Jesus. There was no higher calling than that, and just the thought of it made me feel chosen and good.

All these years later, long after quitting religion altogether, it's difficult to tease out the origin of this one desire from the strands of my childhood. There's no one moment or experience I can recall that kindled it, although a blend of various possibilities could have done the trick. I loved some of the nuns at St. John, especially the young ones like Sr. Gabriel and Sr. David, who were outgoing and vivacious, two qualities for which I hungered. Nuns commanded respect—although not as much as priests—and people deferred to them. From my usual place on the margins of things, being brought into the center was inviting. In our parish, families with a daughter-nun were held in high regard, as was the daughter herself for committing to a life of service in Jesus' name. Terrified of attracting attention to myself, I nevertheless longed to be noticed as the terrific girl beneath those muffling layers of shyness and social clumsiness. Maybe I thought being a nun would free me.

My mother was a faithful Catholic, and my father was particularly devout, so perhaps I thought it would please them. I already tried in my own way to follow in Daddy's religious footsteps by being attentive at Mass, giving up candy every Lent to contribute plenty of nickels and dimes to the missions for pagan babies, and by doing helpful things I could offer up to Jesus, such as going in to school on occasional Saturdays to help the sisters scrub classroom floors.

According to Mom and my sister Jean, our entire family visited a nearby nuns' motherhouse for some special occasion, although my recollection has only Daddy and me there, happy and close. Close to fifty years later, only sparse details of the day linger in my memory: Serene nuns in their black and white habits mingling with happy families dressed in their Sunday best, and everyone walking in a huge, leafy garden that now so distantly shimmers with sunlight and vibrant purpose. Perhaps the sisters were having an open house as a way of attracting more girls to their small high school and older postulants to the order. I can imagine Daddy saying he hoped to send me to the high school someday, and feeling proud as only a little girl can when her dad singles her out for a special honor. I can imagine watching the friendly young nuns-to-be and glowing with the hope of joining them after my father revealed how proud that would make him. And I can imagine searching my heart for something that would make him happy and asking expectantly, "Daddy, do you think I would be a good nun?" to which he replied, "You would be a wonderful nun."

In reality, though, I have no sense that these tender father-daughter conversations are anything more than fantasy. By seventh grade, and probably earlier, my desire to join the convent vanished.

All these decades later, I don't remember why, although I can offer some good guesses.

First of all, I did not have a religious vocation, the Divine spark that infuses the soul with the desire to formally consecrate itself to God. If I had, it would not have trickled away into nothing, never to reappear. So perhaps as I grew older, the idea of convent walls came to feel more confining than protective. Almost a teenager then, perhaps I was beginning to break loose from childish solutions to the pain of feeling nearly mute with shyness when out in the world. But then I wonder, if my desire had sprung mostly from what my heart—or my imagination—believed Daddy wanted or expected of me, did I deliberately change my mind after that day he broke my heart? Because I believed he had turned his back to me, did I turn my back to him? Was whatever indifference I could muster easier to bear than my grief at losing him?

In May 2006, my father had been dead forty years. Having him gone that long felt momentous, and he was often on my mind. By then in my own mid-life and still fascinated with nuns (reading memoirs, for instance, or watching Audrey Hepburn again in *The Nun's Story*), I could understand wanting to be a sister in large part for him. I had loved my dad so much, this ordinary man who had been willing to make great sacrifices to be of service to God and to the suffering human beings he understood were God's children. To my little Catholic girl's heart—unaware of the damage those sacrifices wreaked on his marriage and family, and even on himself—it was a noble thing, something a hero or a saint in one of my books might have done. In unconscious admiration, I wanted to emulate him and make my own noble sacrifice by marrying Jesus, as nuns do, and donning the black and white habit.

Stretching beyond that, here are the deepest strands of this particular story I've been able to tease out. The nuns I loved had consecrated themselves to an ideal, and in my little world they were simply the most obvious symbols of deepest devotion to a heart's call. My own call was still decades away from finding its voice, but already, even without words to explain it, my young self yearned to pledge her life to something larger than herself, even to something sacred.

From what a future friend named my "dreaming dungeon soul," my call, my vocation—whatever it might turn out to be—already was seeking the light. As I later discovered, there are many ways we can devote ourselves to the holy mysteries, however we define them.

•

A fine bit of writing nourishes my spirit more than almost anything. I'm still madly in love with books. Maybe it's lust. Reading books is my only addiction, and buying them is my only spending vice. For years, my library card has languished because owning books means not having to release them, like hostages with whom you've fallen in love. Reading often delights me so much with, say, unexpected insights or the surprise of a perfect metaphor, that if I were a dog, it would set my tail to wagging. Devastated once by a break-up with a lover, I fled to the one place I was sure to find solace—a bookstore—and brought home a memoir (Paul Monette) and two collections of personal essays (Nancy Mairs). Back at home, I flung myself to the couch for three days and soothed myself with the eloquence and honesty of their words.

Back in eighth grade, after I'd progressed from stories about girl detectives Nancy Drew and Trixie Belden to novels like Conrad Richter's pioneer saga, *The Trees*, our class newspaper asked the question, What do you want to be? My answer: A writer. Until that moment, such a thought had never entered my head. I didn't even know if it was true. But it wasn't exactly a lie, either; my answer was more a vague notion of returning the pleasure so many writers had given to me.

That idea lasted about a day. How could I be a writer? They were so creative. I once read a story about a dog who buried ice cubes and later was confused when he couldn't find them. I could never write anything that clever. And writers knew what they wanted to write; their words on the page were evidence of that. I could hardly ever figure out what I wanted to say, let alone write it. Shyness tied my tongue in knots and kept my deepest feelings tucked inside, the ones I couldn't explain to myself, let alone anyone else.

In his book *Callings: Finding and Following an Authentic Life*, Gregg Levoy writes, "The point of passion is mainly to follow, to let yourself love what you love, to respect your hunger and obey your thirst." But first, you have to know what you love, what you hunger and thirst *for*. Sure, I loved reading, thirsted and hungered for words on the page, but how could I make a liv-

ing with that? So, for about fifteen years after college, I supported myself in corporate America. I managed to perform well
enough to meet the expectations of my bosses, and even rose to
middle ranks. None of those jobs nourished me, though.
Instead, I waited to be found out for what I really was: an
imposter in a suit and little heels who was desperate to keep
playing the game because she needed the paycheck. Fortunately,
reading continued to be my joy and my escape.

Then one autumn day in 1987, potential salvation arrived
by way of the morning paper: the local utility company was seeking a public information writer. Whatever that was, it sounded
intriguing, although a total absence of professional writing experience certainly would land my application in the trash. On the
other hand, I was desperate to escape from corporate management. Maybe this ad was an invitation from the universe. As my
dad used to say, "What the hey?"

I remembered a famous cartoon by Sidney Harris that
shows two scientists standing in front of a blackboard on which
one has written a long, complex equation. Linking the two
sections of the equation are the words, "Then a miracle occurs."
A month or so after applying for the job, my miracle occurred,
and it linked the two sections of my life's equation: before
becoming a writer and after. Light streamed into my dungeon as
never before, and I followed my newly freed passion with all my
heart. So what if I was describing power plants and employee
benefits, and ghostwriting executives' speeches and technical
presentations? I consecrated myself to becoming a creative, solid
writer, learning the craft by putting thousands of words on
paper, studying books about writing well, attending workshops
and classes, and as always, absorbing elements of good writing
through the osmosis of reading, reading, reading. Soon, co-
workers and executives told me the company had never had a

better-written employee news magazine.

But after four years there, my idea of hell was writing that damn magazine every month for all eternity. Corporate communications was confining, relentlessly one-sided, and repetitive. Instead of following my passion, I now was flogging it to death, one press release, one shareholder brochure at a time. A bit of freelancing for local publications offered me small opportunities to break out. For my first freelance article, about an 11-year-old gymnast and for which I zealously over-prepared, the *Evansville Sports Journal* paid all of $35 (and spelled my name wrong in the byline), but local libraries carried the small paper. People could read my writing in the library! When my boss later forbade me to freelance because my writing was supposed to be representing only the utility company, I used a pen name and she never knew.

Once exciting and empowering, my miracle job had become a prison of boredom, and also of company values in which I didn't believe, old-fashioned presumed male superiority, and the wrath of my poor boss, who, trapped in the much same way I was, launched her frustration on the staff.

Every day, the terrazzo floor in the hallway outside my office telegraphed her mood, her two-inch heels on the marble-like surface sending advance warning. Sharp, tense clicks tapped out *Escape while you can!* Slower, softer footfalls meant *You're safe for the moment.* Unfortunately, I believed there was no escape, neither from her nor from the job. Single and with no other income, how would I support myself without returning to management duties and life as an impostor? As my anxiety wound tighter and tighter over my final two years there, my body was telegraphing its own message: Get out or suffer the consequences.

I suffered.

First came the depression. It was like walking around

with rocks in my pockets. In the beginning, they disappeared outside working hours, but then they grew and weighed me down all the time. My stomach grew so jittery with tension, I could not eat much and had to safety-pin waistbands to hold up my skirts. In dreams, I turned to ice or wandered, bewildered, in a shifting, ugly environment.

Then came the hammering pain in my head. Brain scans discovered no visible reason for it, which, not surprisingly, happened only at work. Then one day, feeling pummeled by a string of dreadful-boss days and fearing the afternoon, the week, the rest of my working life in that place, another headache started creeping in. Only this time, I refused to let it happen. I sat quietly at my desk, breathing slowly and scanning my body for clues about what was going on. There it was: clearly, I could feel the muscles in my scalp and face begin to tighten in a viselike grip. By constantly clamping down my emotions at work—*I am a professional! I must not break down in sobs!*—I was creating the headaches without realizing it. So I experimented and found that consciously relaxing those muscles let the pain ebb away. Amazing. With practice, I learned to do this every time a headache appeared, and they vanished for good.

But since I was still embroiled in an impossible situation, the tension didn't disappear. It just headed slightly south. My neck and shoulder muscles tightened so severely I couldn't turn my head. Trying to look over my shoulder meant twisting my entire upper body from the waist. Loosening those muscles took a month of twice-weekly physical therapy sessions. Several years later, I was flipping through my journal from this time in early 1993, full of complaints about the job and laments about my poor neck, and discovered a line that made me yelp in recognition: "Think I'll just sit tight until something better comes along."

Sit tight, indeed. When I wrote those words, they were merely a defeated end to that particular bout of woe-dumping. But my subconscious knew the score and delivered up the perfect metaphor. If only I'd had the awareness to listen at the time. But the miracle job was collapsing all around me, and I was too busy dodging the falling shards. Fear of staying, fear of leaving—how could I choose?

When we become aware of the passionate stirring, the calling Levoy identifies, we must listen for its faint voice struggling to be heard through the chaos with which we've surrounded ourselves. If we ignore it, it grows louder and more rebellious until it forces us to pay attention. Then we must try to understand as it defines itself, often a tricky proposition because we know that whatever shape it takes will not fit into the life we're already living. Furthermore, we understand that responding fully will likely cause us pain. In following a call, we must often leave precious treasures behind—loved ones or a home, cherished beliefs, a source of income, or habits and things that comfort us—as we strike out in search of new and different ones. This is the barrier as well as the lure.

In August 1993 my calling's faintest voice guided me to a women's writing conference at Skidmore College in Saratoga Springs, New York. My only goal was to enjoy the camaraderie of other writers and perhaps write something fun and creative. Instead, I ended up plotting my escape from the utility company. The women there—some of them full-time freelance writers— rescued me with their own stories of possibilities and hope. It is possible to survive and even thrive as a freelancer, they said: All you need is belief and a plan. So I made plans and figured belief would tag along later. Even before boarding the plane home, I knew how to liberate myself from the utility company. After the satisfying early years of writing there, the pain and difficulty of the final two years had done their job: Pound me hard enough and long enough, rather like a Sherman tank, to persuade me to quit and risk following my call. Fear of not having a steady income had rooted me in place, and only such a pounding could have shoved me out of a "secure" job and into a freelance life of playing with words.

After several months of laying groundwork, I gave a month's notice. In January 1994, I was a full-time freelance writer; my new business card called me The Word Worker. Despite the financial risk, which paled in comparison to the danger that remaining on the job posed to my physical and emotional health, I trusted and jumped off the cliff, as the saying goes, praying to grow wings before the *splat*!

Amazingly, another miracle occurred: my plan worked. Nearly fifteen years later, it's still chugging along, having undergone revisions as necessary. For nearly the first ten years of that time, until I remarried, I supported myself solely through freelance writing. At first, most of my income came from writing marketing materials for local businesses; I'd met many business owners through the utility company, and they referred me to others. I did proofreading and copyediting. With more freelancing for local publications under my belt, I gradually broke into bigger magazines as planned. I also wrote short nonfiction books about subjects such as military-unit and county history, and contributed to others. The book you're now reading is my first collection of personal essays, a genre I came to cherish after that healing weekend of reading Nancy Mairs. "I want to grub around in the roots connecting experience with belief and action," she wrote. I second that.

Words are holy things: By giving us voice, they allow us

to transcend the mute isolation inside our own heads. Without words for self-expression, who are we? Without words, how could I tell you about the pair of red-headed woodpeckers with their black and white-striped wings sitting in the scarlet-leaved oak outside my window this very minute, the whole scene brilliant with sun? Or about the isolation of shyness that kept me tongue-knotted as a kid and lured me to the written words of others and the gifts they offered? How could you tell me about the miracle of your new baby son or your grief at the death of your mother, or even about the tuna sandwich you had for lunch?

Words that arise with coherence and beauty on the page, that's the holy mystery I serve. Like the nuns devoted to God, on my best days writing lets me serve something larger than myself: human self-expression that occasionally touches someone else's heart and brings us closer together.

Whether it's serving God or writing essays, building boats or raising children, every call arises from passion. Surprisingly, I've found this passion to be nurtured by many unexpected sources: a career that does not fit, feeling so stuck you can move only if you learn to fly, people who make you crazy, situations that hurt so much you want to die. The key is taking the time and finding the strength to listen to what these things are telling you.

Unlike the nuns' call, mine is not religious, but it's sacred nonetheless. I am blessed by having allowed myself to follow it. My deepest heart keeps tugging me toward this satisfying, happily painful struggle to communicate truthfully using the written word. Over and over again, my call crooks its finger at me, luring me to another place lush with promise and ripe with passion: to an unexpected phrase that delights me as it flows slippery and easy from my heart to the page; to the instant when all the vague, jumbled thoughts taunting me just out of conscious reach glide into clear, occasionally eloquent, prose; and even to getting paid for reading, as I often must do in preparation for writing.

How can I, as a writer and a human being, resist? Roused from my sleepwalk and finally on my way home, what else can I do but follow my call, full of trust and desire?

CHAPTER THREE
Overcoming the Wobblies, or Those are the Brakes

There I stood, convinced I would die in this Atlanta parking lot for love of a man who loved bicycles. He was so passionate about cycling that, every spring, he shaved the curly, blonde hair off his muscular legs and kept them smooth all summer, like the pros do. I hadn't been on a bike in probably 25 years; in fact, I'd never actually learned to ride. But I didn't want him to pedal off into the sunset without me, either, so I decided to try again. For love, I thought, I can do this. Off to the bike shop we drove, where we chose a 12-speed Cannondale for my test drive. It was sleek, expensive, and very cool.

In the neighborhood where I grew up, curbside elms arched across the wide streets to create soft, leafy tunnels in the summer. Dads and moms heading home from factories or grocery shopping drove slowly, keeping an eye out for playing kids. As soon as the first warm days teased opened doors shut tight all winter, kids were out on their bikes, pedaling up and down our street and the alley running alongside our house. It looked like fun.

But it was scary, too: You could crash. Jumping rope was safer. I was good at that, especially double Dutch, and it was fun doing cartwheels and somersaults on the lawn dotted with dandelions, and pretend-galloping my stallion with the flowing mane and tail down the sidewalk, hands pulling back on imaginary reins when he needed a breather. And reading was the most fun of all.

Daddy brought home my first bicycle when I was maybe six. I don't remember asking for a bike, but perhaps one day I felt brave, or saw from the big front window how fun and free it looked to pedal in packs around the neighborhood. In the style of the day, my bike was sturdy and chunky, with coaster brakes. I stopped it by pushing a foot backwards and down on one of the pedals. It had pale green fenders with white trim, and the tires were fat, about three inches wide. With training wheels attached, it was easy to ride, even though I wasn't very good at balancing: pedal, tip to one side, the little click of a training wheel hitting the sidewalk, upright again, pedal, tip to the other side, click, come back up, wobble down the block past the Sypults' house and the Webbers', and maybe even past the Piekniews', six houses down from ours. Every once in a while, when neither training wheel touched for several seconds and my bike seemed to glide, I felt as light as if released from gravity. Bike riding was fun as long as I didn't think about crashing. Which I always did.

But I couldn't be a baby forever. The training wheels had to come off eventually. Daddy convinced me it would be okay. I wasn't so sure. He promised to hold on to the seat and help me stay up.

And he did. For a while. As wobbly as a novice tightrope walker, I pedaled down the middle of Maplewood Avenue, Daddy trotting alongside me and gripping the back of the pale-green leather seat. *Oh! I can't steer. The handlebars won't go straight. If Daddy lets go, I'll fall. It will really hurt if I fall on the street. I'm so scared. I want my training wheels back. I can't go straight, and the bike's all tippy and I'm going to fall. This is too hard. My stomach hurts.*

Little tears began leaking from my eyes, but Daddy couldn't see, and I didn't want to be a baby so I kept pedaling. "You're doing great!" he said. "Keep going!" I grew more scared and my stomach hurt more and he let go and I pedaled a few feet further then couldn't steer the bike and couldn't stop either and my front tire hit the curb and I crashed.

Daddy came running over, and now I don't remember if I even so much as skinned my knee. But that didn't matter. That out-of-control, tipping, falling feeling left me sobbing. I never wanted to feel like that again. A few days later, Daddy convinced me to try a few more times, and wanting to be brave, I did. The results were the same, though: too wobbly…too scary…crash.

A few years later, I decided it was dumb that I couldn't ride a bike. Anybody could ride a bike. So Daddy bought me another one. It was beautiful, copper-colored and blue, with thinner tires and still only one gear and coaster brakes. I practiced in the street near the house for a few days, and wobbled but stayed upright and could steer pretty straight. To stop, a little backward push on the pedal always did the trick. Feeling brave one day, I decided to ride to Nancy's house a few blocks away. Off to a good start but still a little shaky, I wasn't prepared for that bump in the sidewalk. Panicked as the front wheel veered wildly, I lost control and fell. Some boys on their bikes nearby howled with laughter. I walked my beautiful bike home, where it joined the old green one in the garage.

Decades later, I embarked on a relationship with this near-fanatical cyclist. He lived in Southern Indiana, only seven hours away by car from Atlanta, so we began visiting back and forth several weekends a month. Which is how I came to be in that parking lot.

Inside, I felt as wobbly as during that first training wheel-free ride on my little green bike. The shaking in my hands reached all the way down to my knees. The vehicle upon which I was about to sacrifice myself had neither fat tires nor coaster brakes. What it did possess were hand brakes nearly out of my reach on the downward-curving handlebars. Visions of crashing skittered through my mind. *Oh, stop it,* I reprimanded myself. *You're not a little kid any more.*

While my Significant Other held the Cannondale steady, I gingerly climbed on, certain of my doom. Not daring to use the toe clips, I flipped the pedals upside down and rolled across the gently sloping parking lot. Terrified, I couldn't steer; I didn't know enough to lean my body into the direction I wanted to turn. Even though I was headed toward the broadside of a parked car, the thought of using the hand brakes never crossed my mind. I just kept jamming the pedals backward uselessly, confused about why the bike didn't stop. As if in slow motion, I crashed into the car. Since I was hardly speeding, no damage resulted to car, bike, or body. But the embarrassment was excruciating.

Later that day at another shop, I bought a bike, figuring I'd eventually learn to ride it. S.O. never said so, but I knew that riding was crucial to this relationship. He rode scores of miles every week and often went on weekend group rides. He practically rode in his sleep. If I didn't ride, what would we do together? This relationship looked to be the most promising one since my divorce more than a decade earlier. I was going to ride a damn bike.

I tried. My apartment complex near Atlanta was a good place to practice—not much traffic, picturesque grounds with a winding road, some hills. Helmeted and gloved, I'd go out after work, steeled to the task. Just like on the Cannondale, the brakes were nearly out of reach, and it was nerve-wracking to take one hand off the handlebars to reach down and shift; it threw my already precarious balance out of whack. I did slide my feet into the toe clips because that helped with efficient peddling, but that made me nervous, too—what if I had to put my foot down really fast to stop from falling over? Which I did—a lot. How humiliating.

After moving to Indiana to live with this man who had bicycle chains for sinews, I kept trying to ride, but neither my fears nor my cycling skills improved. Naturally, this created a bit of tension around our house. During one argument I explained how, from childhood, I'd been afraid of being hurt while riding and couldn't seem to get past that. His response was to ask if I'd ever broken a bone, which he'd done many times.

"No," I replied.

"It's not so bad," he said.

Not exactly the compassionate response for which I'd hoped.

Fortunately, S.O. also owned a tandem, which he had purchased with his former wife. This machine was a sleek, yellow Mercian from France, with disk brakes and more than twenty gears—both important safety measures when moving and stopping 300 rolling pounds. He said tandems were called "divorce machines" because couples often could not coordinate their riding styles, leading to much frustration and unpleasant-ness. His former wife, he said, always leaned the wrong way when going around a turn and didn't want to peddle hard enough on the uphills. But in the two years S.O. and I were together, I became an accomplished stoker, the one who rode in back. The person in front was the captain, and S.O. did an excel-lent job. He shifted gears, braked, and guided us through traffic as we pedaled in sweet unison. My leg muscles grew strong and sleek, and before too long a twenty-mile ride through hilly Southern Indiana was too short to offer much of a challenge. I leaned easily into turns just the right amount at the right time (thanks to lessons years before from a boyfriend who sometimes carried me around on the back of his motorcycle). With no nerve-wracking decisions to make, I just pedaled like the dickens, relished the exercise, and soaked up the scenery. Plunging down hills at 45 mph set us to whooping (even as I prayed we wouldn't hit a hole or bump in the pavement), and there was no greater joy than having the wind at our backs on the flats, our pedaling rhythmic and strong.

S.O. always said I was the best tandem partner, but that was not enough to keep us together. When after two years we broke up and he moved away, I was grounded, missing not only him, but also the happiness of riding in tandem.

Dwight was a serious cyclist, too. Riding the tandem had hooked me, so by this time, I was ready to master cycling on my own. Even though I'd never ridden well without a partner, I still craved that surge of my own physical strength, feeling the push of my leg muscles as they hoisted me up hills, followed by the release and exhilaration of the downhill rush. Now that a new teacher had appeared, this 38-year-old student was ready. Dwight found a used Motobecane for me, and we scheduled our first lesson for one evening after work.

Merely thinking about riding solo stirred up the old queasiness, but this time I was prepared. Sitting quietly on the couch before Dwight arrived, with eyes closed and breath slowed, I visualized riding the way I wanted to ride. Since my greatest fear was falling, I needed something to hold me up. A skyhook. A big red hook descending behind me from the sky that slipped under the equally imaginary belt around my waist as I rode. No way could I fall with my trusty skyhook in place. The scene unfolded in my imagination, its chemical tendrils extending through my brain, which produced calming internal juices and quieted my racing heart and jumpy stomach. As I rode confidently through the Indiana countryside of my mind, my skyhook absorbed all my fear.

Dwight wisely decided that my first lesson should happen far from traffic and other distractions, so he drove us to a new highway bypass, nearly complete and still closed to vehicles. As he unloaded the Motobecane from the back of his pickup, visions of broken bones—my broken bones—skittered through my mind. Even if S.O. believed they weren't so bad, I didn't agree. Breaking a bone would hurt like hell.

Take a deep breath. Think skyhook.

I managed to work my feet into the toe clips and, rather unsteadily, took off. Gripping the handlebars so tightly my hands slowly went numb, I rolled along the brand-new concrete on two skinny wheels, awkward and terrified that I'd have to shift or brake suddenly. Occasionally, though, I felt myself gliding effort-lessly, perfectly balanced and graceful. When the wobblies threatened, I visualized my skyhook supporting me.

Amazingly, it worked. We rode five miles up, five miles back. Not very fast, but Dwight was patient.

Back at the truck, I felt as proud, and as exhausted, as if I'd won the Tour de France. Dwight smiled wide and rewarded me with a hearty, "You did it!" We scheduled another lesson.

Back at the new bypass several days later, skyhook at the ready, I wasn't prepared for the direction Dwight took. We rode for several miles on the bypass, but then, way ahead, he headed for an exit ramp. Big yellow-and-black striped barricades weight-ed down with sandbags blocked the passage of four-wheeled vehicles. The opening between them was maybe four feet wide, but sandbags on the ground narrowed the path for my wheels even further. I would become the thread passing through the needle's eye, and the seamstress had the shakes. Oh, God—there was *gravel* down there, just where I'd have to make a sharp right turn to avoid hurtling into the busy traffic on the cross street. As fear demolished my skyhook, panic unleashed my childhood habits: I forgot to use the hand brakes to slow down. So I did the next best thing—flying between the barricades, I grabbed the one to my left.

I came to an abrupt halt and gravity dumped me to the concrete as the bike lurched forward alone, then teetered and fell over on the gravel. Dwight saw it all as he waited at the bottom of the ramp for me to catch up. He did his best not to laugh too hard. After a minute, I stood up and brushed off the seat of my black bike shorts. The slammed blood vessels in my hip were already ganging up for a brilliant bruise.

For a minute or two, I wanted to quit riding. My little maneuver was so embarrassing. But then I realized I'd fallen off my bike and survived—and with no broken bones or any harm beyond leaving a large portion of my dignity on the ramp. Except for a lost peddle reflector, my bike was undamaged. I climbed stiffly back in the saddle, a little shaky but beginning to laugh at my goofy, albeit effective, stopping technique. We rode back to the truck.

Dwight soon installed straight handlebars on my bike, along with shifters I could maneuver with my thumbs and brakes right there within my reach—I never had to take my hands off the bars to ride well. These modifications made all the difference. Three months later, I rode a grueling seventy-mile trip with him and two of his friends. At one point, sheer exhaustion made me cry; I'd hit the wall. The three guys teased me, but I didn't care. I wasn't afraid anymore.

Finally, at age 38, I could ride a bike.

Learning to simultaneously ride and drink from my water

bottle took some time to master, and tight, fast U-turns gave me pause for a while. However, operating hand brakes became second nature, and the skyhook had performed its job so well that I retired it.

Dwight and I didn't date for very long, but we remained friends and drove together to a couple of big group rides that first summer and fall after I began riding. At one ride in Northern Kentucky, we ran into S.O. and his new girlfriend, C. (later to become his wife). S.O. looked surprised when he spotted me in the registration line.

"You won't believe it," I said, feeling proud of myself, "but I'm not a total klutz after all. I'm riding my own bike now."

"That's great," he said, with some surprise. "I'm glad for you."

Then he introduced me to C., whom I'd heard about through the grapevine. A long-time cyclist very active in the local bike club, she was a pleasant woman with dark, curly hair. I felt a little inferior in comparison, still being slightly nervous on my own two wheels, and sad, too, knowing he now preferred her to me.

The next morning after a hearty breakfast designed to begin fueling us for the ride, hundreds of cyclists took off for the day's fifty miles. Somewhere along the way, as my quadriceps burned in the struggle to propel me up the low grade of a never-ending hill, S.O. and C. flew past me on the Mercian, he the captain of course, and she occupying my former seat as the stoker. Wearing matching bike shorts and jerseys, they laughed and hollered encouragement to one another. Their feet circled in the steady, coupled rhythm of a tandem, and as they stood up in the pedals for extra power, their muscular legs pumped seemingly with little effort. Working together to reach the crest, their joy was evident. I blinked a few times to hold back tears.

Several minutes later, my lungs burning and my thighs quivering with the effort, I reached the top of the hill and coasted for a few moments to catch my breath. Then, exhilarated at my solo accomplishment, I hunkered down over the handlebars to reduce wind resistance and prepared to revel in the swooping rush of the downhill.

CHAPTER FOUR
Fallow Time (1998)

Faint light is leaking through the bedroom mini-blinds, but there's no good reason to get out of bed. It's late winter in Southern Indiana. The sodden ground is blotched with dirty patches of snow, and wilted lawns droop, defeated under ashen clouds that have hung overhead for weeks. The two Chinese maples outside the windows of my second-story apartment are for half the year emerald and leafy with life, but now they stand skeletal against the sky.

Late last year, Mom was diagnosed with breast cancer. Her words—"It's malignant"—floated through the phone line directly to my heart. The world tilted and I slipped towards the edge. My mother, the only true constant in my life, who would always love me no matter what, would die. Maybe not from this, but from something. Now, months later, her treatment seems to have worked, but I'm still reeling from the gut-level realization that my mom is mortal: someday I will have to continue without her. Just over a year ago, my sister Jean's husband, Tim, did die unexpectedly at a young age, and in the face of her grief, I feel useless and ham-handed in my attempts at comfort. I've been sick myself with small illnesses one after another that have left me dismal and off-balance for weeks on end. Divorced for two decades, I've also been dateless for months and months. The shock of the last man leaving nearly did me in, and stumbling around again in the cavernous loneliness, I can find no place of repose. Even my women friends are busy with their own lives and seem too busy to include me very often.

My work isn't going so well, either. When I left my corporate writing job to freelance, I had visions of writing more than marketing brochures and company newsletters. Sure, they pay the bills and serve a purpose, and more magazine assignments are trickling in. But it all feels flat somehow, not nearly as satisfying as I'd envisioned. Lately, without the energy or motivation to seek out more challenging, satisfying jobs, I'm working way too hard for way too little money, writing on autopilot and churning out writing I don't much care about except for the money it fetches. And even that has been faltering as promised jobs or hoped-for assignments fall through.

All the juice has seeped through the cracks in my life, leaving me brittle as a husk. I need to rest, please, just rest, and not have painful demands or terrible surprises visited upon me for a long time so my weary heart can regain its balance.

Once again this morning, it's as if too much gravity pushes down on me, making movement difficult. It would be easier to just remain here, immobile under the blankets. But I have things to do, so I lure myself out of bed with the promise of hot tea. It's not much, but it offers a small promise of comfort and warmth. Heat chugs out of the radiators, but in the old building with its poor insulation, it's chilly nevertheless. I wrap my heavy robe over my flannel nightgown, pull on slippers over the socks I've slept in, and head for the kitchen. The apartment is small, so it's not far. The vertical blinds in the living room and kitchen are still closed, cocooning my possessions in the dim light. I hear my neighbor Grace moving around in the apartment below.

While a mug of water heats in the microwave and a bag of English Breakfast waits on the counter, I open the blinds in the big kitchen window. A bit of sun breaking through the overcast hits the maples outside like a spotlight, and the sight startles me: Little rubies are glistening against the trees' damp, gray bark. When did they pop out? Based on the size of the red buds, it was days ago.

I pull the blinds all the way back and crank open the casement window over the table. Widening sunlight and the fresh, cold air wash over my face as I look closer at the buds. How could I have missed them? But there they are, dazzling in the surprisingly golden morning, right at eye level as though I lived in a tree house. I stand there, awed. And in the millisecond it takes for that rosy picture to splash from my optic nerve to my brain, my locked-down heart swirls open a little, just enough to spark the hope that still lingers there. Small but real, it's enough. It can lead me out. I know what to do.

Ding! goes the microwave. I put the teabag in the hot water and sit the mug on the kitchen table, feeling purposeful for the first time in ages. In the living room, I dig through the near-permanent pile of magazines and books at one end of the couch to unearth my buried journal. I notice how all the books are memoirs and personal essays. That makes sense—I've been reading to find out how other people cope with the difficulties of their lives.

Now, though, it's time to take a shot at discovering how to cope with mine.

Back at the kitchen table, so close to the trees I could caress branch tips through the window, my pen flies across the spiral-bound pages of my journal, filling each line from end to end, each page from top to bottom, hardly able to keep up with the flow of words. This act of writing down uncensored thoughts, meant for no eyes but mine, is terrifically liberating—a fact I'd forgotten, or squelched, a while back, when some new punch to the gut had finally been too much even to record. I write without the usual constraints—grammar, precision, editing, *is it good enough?* The only rule is to keep the pen moving no matter what, following the river of words that dredges up little gifts from my subconscious, those nuggets enclosing the real treasures buried under all the muck.

Somewhere in all the scribbling, the knowledge I have been searching for all these months flows from pen to page: "I am stuck." This simple realization is so obvious, I laugh and stop writing for a moment. But it's perfect. It's the chink in the mortar that starts the whole wall tumbling.

"I am stuck"—I know exactly where this nugget comes from. Over the years, I'd read Robert Pirsig's *Zen and the Art of Motorcycle Maintenance* several times, drawn back to it again and again, and each time understood more. In 1993, Pirsig's words about being stuck helped me make the break into freelance writing. At a time when I was stuck firmly in the belief that the only way to support myself was to be an employee of some company, they gave me the courage to liberate myself from a writing job that riddled me with anxiety. Pirsig believed that being stuck was actually a wonderful place to be: It's "the predecessor of all real understanding," he wrote.

This morning, I know how right he is.

When we're mired in the muck, it's because we've exhausted all our usual options. The feeling of stuckness comes from applying traditional thinking and behavior to new situations and having them not work, repeatedly. The only way to free ourselves is to try something new.

I begin writing again, more blue ink curling even faster onto the journal page. A possible solution appears: "Maybe instead of going forward or backward, right or left, it's time to go up or down. Time to fly or to retreat to the depths for a while to see what you can find there."

I'm not ready to fly just yet, weighed down with this emotional baggage I do not quite know how to release or otherwise handle. But the notion of retreat is appealing. Not giving up, but simply being quiet, going fallow for a time and understanding that this is not my season for planting but for simply remembering how new life is always stirring beneath the surface, no matter what's going on up top.

Several well-meaning friends have suggested I "take something" to feel better. Certainly, drugs can be a godsend for people with true severe depression. But my sadness or melancholy or grief is not clinical depression—it's a normal, even healthy, response to all the painful situations of late. I want to feel *all* my emotions, not bury the difficult ones under a pavement of unnecessary drugs where they can flourish like toxic mold. Dealing with them directly might strengthen or nourish me for the future. I'm not a martyr; Thomas Moore's eloquent book, *Care of the Soul: A Guide for Cultivating Depth and Sacredness in Everyday Life*, explained this to me several years ago. "The soul presents itself in a variety of colors," he wrote, "including all the shades of gray, blue, and black. To care for the soul, we must observe the full range of all its colorings, and resist the temptation to approve of only white, red, and orange—the brilliant colors." From Moore I had learned that painful feelings can lead to a place of transformation, if only we can accept, even embrace, them as part of the human experience.

Several years ago, my best friend's husband deserted her for another woman. The betrayal pierced Lynda so deeply, she feared she'd go crazy with it. After taking an antidepressant for a short time, she could sense that her most profound emotions were sealed beneath the surface. Even though she needed to express them in order to heal, she couldn't *not* feel good. So she stopped taking the drug. In the end, what helped her most was expressing the dark colors of her soul. With the blessing of her counselor, she began to say whatever was on her mind, wherever she was. In all innocence, a smiling grocery cashier would ask, "And how are you today?" Lynda would reply honestly, sometimes with tears, taking several minutes to explain her devastation. "He cheated on me with his secretary for a long time," Lynda would say. "And then he left me to go live with her." The stunned clerk would look embarrassed for this bereft woman in front of her, but Lynda would leave the store relieved for her honest revelation. Later, she said this was one of the best things she did for her recovery.

I stop writing to sip my tea, and it's cool. As it warms in the microwave, I stretch and wiggle my fingers after clutching my pen and writing hard for nearly half an hour. I realize what a fierce grip I've been keeping on my emotions all these months, fighting so hard to appear normal and keep on in the same way I always had, despite the emotional pounding.

Yes, that's the reason I've been so shrouded in pain: It's not my fear of losing Mom or the grief over my sister's loss, or my own loneliness and disappointment that have been weighing me down so much as my resistance to acknowledging those emotions. So often I say, "I'm fine," when in fact I'm desolate. Unlike Lynda, I haven't been brave enough to drop the façade. That's what has left me stuck and walled in.

Under this onslaught of one crisis after another, my life right now isn't painted in Moore's brilliant colors at all. But denying my darker-hued feelings has only increased the pain. There's a saying, "What we resist, persists." The rest I need, my time for going fallow, will begin when I simply accept that I'm in pain, and that being in pain is a perfectly acceptable, even necessary, part of being human.

With my now-warm tea, I sit down again at the table but not to write. My journaling today has done its job and feels complete for now. So I sit back to relax, hands cupped around the warm mug, and again look out the kitchen window.

Those maple buds have blessed me with their rosy grace. Every year, they sprout and grow, then fall and go fallow, and then they start all over again. I declare this my fallow time, for as long as it takes. Healthy transformation will not be possible unless I give it time to root itself, down deep in the moistness and the quiet and the dark. Rejuvenated by the simple movement of pen on paper, I am no longer fighting my emotions. Instead, I will honor them, allowing whatever transformation awaits to take hold.

CHAPTER FIVE
Always Enough

It was absolutely the bravest thing I'd ever done. Now I had to make it work—or end up pushing my trusty Macintosh around Evansville in a pilfered shopping cart.

Leaving Corporate America and a $30,000 salary behind, I stepped off the cliff into a life of freelance writing. The median income for that profession was said to be only $7,000, but surely I could do better than that. In any case, I would be careful with the money that did flow my way.

By working at home, my expenses decreased automatically: no more expensive suits, no commuting expenses, far fewer lunches out. While still employed and writing a few free-lance articles on the side, I'd bought a boxy, little Macintosh computer and inkjet printer, which now sat on the desk in my small living room. My other desk—a roll-top so impractical in the computer age—had been sacrificed to fund the purchase of a thermal fax machine, now atop a new filing cabinet. In   addition, the rent on my cozy apartment was only $325, my faithful Corolla was long since paid off, and my medical insurance was only $80 a month. Self-discipline and persever-ance, supplemented by a huge amount of grace, would do the trick.

On January 3, 1994, my new adventure got off to an excel-lent start. My former boss had contracted with me to continue

writing the next two issues of the employee news magazine—
at $2,000 a pop!—while she searched for my replacement.
Businesspeople I'd met through the corporate writing job asked
me to write brochures and newsletters (and they later referred
me to other businesses). On many of these jobs I partnered
with Lynda, who had her own home-based graphics design
business. None of these projects was great literature, but they
required creativity and kept me free of corporate shackles while
I broke into magazines. A freelance magazine editor in town
began   funneling article assignments paying several hundred
dollars apiece my way. The *Evansville Courier* and other local
publications ran my feature stories. They didn't pay much, but
the clips were important proof of my writing ability for bigger
markets.

Who needs a regular paycheck? I thought. This freelance
gig was going to be a snap.

I started working for a paycheck at age 16. George and
Vi Madvek hired me to work weekends at Madvek's Vienna
Red Hots, in Hammond, Indiana, serving up those all-beef
hot dogs, fries, Polish sausages, tacos, and soft drinks. It was a
small restaurant, with half-a-dozen stools at the counter
and three tables. The heat from the steam table fogged the plate-
glass   windows on cold winter nights. Madvek's was popular
with high school kids, and the jukebox often blared with hits of
the late '60s. Twenty years after working there, hearing "Mony
Mony" by Tommy James and the Shondells blaring from a radio
catapulted me back to Madvek's by my nose—the song yanked
up from my olfactory memory the pungent aroma of all those
fried, grilled, spicy foods often laden with mustard, sauerkraut,
relish, or chili.

Throughout the rest of high school and most of college, I

worked part-time in food service. Later, a degree in Radio/Television/Film Production didn't produce any work, and after my divorce, the corporate world in California provided decent jobs with benefits. From auto insurance rater, I moved up to supervisor, got fired (that should have been a clue), was hired elsewhere as a supervisor and then promoted to regional administrative manager and transferred to Atlanta. I had my own office with a door, which soon provided a convenient place to hide: managing people was never part of my "skill set," and though I did my best, it wasn't enough. I finally had embodied the Peter Principle—people tend to rise to their level of incompetence—but fortunately, love swept me off my feet before I could get fired. I resigned and moved to Evansville, Indiana, in 1987 to live with my new love, the cyclist. There, by some amazing blessing, the local utility company hired me as a corporate writer, even though I had no formal writing experience. My new beau lasted only two years, but during my six years at the utility, I learned to write well on a professional level.

The one constant in all these jobs was a regular paycheck. Every week or two, Big Daddy forked over a piece of paper representing X amount of dollars in return for my services rendered, whether that was scrubbing burned-on grease off the grill, hiring new employees, or writing a speech for the CEO. And that piece of paper, for which I was grateful, paid for all my needs and some of my desires.

Now, though, at age 42, I was my own boss and totally responsible for bringing home the bacon as well as rustling it up in the first place.

Writers' magazines I studied recommended that would-be freelancers collect at least six months' income before taking the plunge. Total self-support could take a long time, if ever, they warned. But saving that amount of money would have taken me years, and I was desperate to ditch corporate life. While my small retirement fund offered a fallback if absolutely necessary, my approach to career liberation was not one I would recommend to anyone else. Fortunately, with no dependents to care for, I was the only one who would suffer should I fail.

"You're so brave to do this," people said, sometimes with a touch of envy. "But how do you keep working without a boss looking over your shoulder?"

"Impending starvation is a great motivator," I usually replied, only half joking.

After my first few exhilarating and lucrative months of freelancing, some ongoing assignments ended, and had not yet been replaced. When April rolled around, I felt prepared for my first-ever quarterly tax payment. Jim, my accountant, came by with the completed forms. He sat on the couch, and I sat down in my chair at the desk across the room and happily spun around to face him.

"Looks like you enjoy being self-employed," he said.

"It's great. I love it! Leaving that last job was the best thing I ever did."

And then the numbers floated out of his mouth, and he might as well have punched me in the gut. My tax bill was at least $1,000 more than I had anticipated.

"Are you all right?" Jim asked.

My stomach hurt. "I don't know."

"It's usually the Social Security taxes that people forget when they start working for themselves," explained Jim. "Employers pay half. But now you're paying the whole thing."

"No, I knew that." The reality of freelancing dumped itself into my lap. "I saved part of every check and thought I had enough. The rest can come out of checking, but that was supposed to cover rent and bills coming up."

"I'm sorry."

Unlike the old employment days, the arrival of checks was never predictable now, especially from magazines, which could take months to pay. And, I'll admit, receiving $2,000 checks with no taxes removed had made me a little giddy; it felt more like a gift—free money!—than payment. That's probably why I hadn't saved more. In any case, I would be squeaking by until someone paid up, and then I would need to find more and more work, forever.

"If it will help, you can pay me later on," Jim offered. His fee was $200.

"Thanks. I really appreciate that."

Unlike my inability to manage employees, I had immense talent for agonizing over trouble that hadn't arrived yet. Give me the slightest opportunity to even anticipate missing a bill payment or two, and I envisioned myself slurping soup at the homeless shelter. When my fears really galloped, that soup was clear broth because all my teeth had fallen out after not being able to afford dental visits for years and years.

So for several nights after Jim delivered the bad news, the skeleton of my starving bank account clattered through my sleepless head. Would my outstanding invoices be paid in time to save me? What if my good luck at finding work evaporated? My landlord was a very nice man, but would his not-so-friendly wife make him throw me out if I missed a rent payment? I teared up at the thought of having to leave my sweet little apartment at the Spring Haven, with the maples in the front yard now large enough to fill my windows with greenery. What if bill collectors started harassing me, and my solid credit rating crumbled? What if my checks started bouncing and I had to endure the narrow-eyed stares of the tellers at my bank—*there's the deadbeat*, they would silently sneer as I walked through the glass and metal doors.

Mom had always been able to budget like nobody's business. A child of the Depression and widowed in 1966 with five young children to raise on the monthly $400 from Daddy's veteran's and Social Security benefits, her skills with a budget were like The Flying Wallendas' on the high wire. She made sure we always had enough food and decent clothing. She paid the mortgage on the house Daddy had built with his brothers. She was able to pay Dr. Peach for regular eye exams and glasses for her five nearsighted children, and we also had regular dental visits. Somehow, she stretched and guarded the available money and made her budget work.

I must have inherited at least some of her budgeting skills. Despite never balancing my check book—working with numbers makes me twitchy and irritable—I was careful to always maintain a safe reserve. And while never committing an actual budget to paper, I knew in my head what my approximate expenses would be. Like Mom, if my car insurance was due every six months, I saved one-sixth of the payment each month. I used my credit card but not extravagantly—well, not usually. And now I saved for taxes, too (and would immediately begin saving more). So money management was not a problem. It was the freelance life I coveted, with its irregular payment, uncertain work, and details like the occasional client who didn't pay or whose checks bounced, or new magazines that folded before paying their writers.

Lynda, Madonna, and I—all freelancers—often commiserated about the financial perils of self-employment.

"Maybe we should just go flip burgers," Madonna said. Taking an afternoon off, we were at Lynda's house, celebrating our freedom with a glass of wine. "At least it would be a steady paycheck."

Lynda and I agreed with the last part of her comment, but then in unison we three chimed, "Nah," and laughed.

"Maybe at gun point."

"Please, shoot me." We were still laughing.

"May none of us ever have to go to a 'real job' again," I added and raised my wineglass.

"That's for sure," said Lynda as Madonna nodded, and both raised their glasses, too.

So "flipping burgers" became our code for any dreadful, drone-like work, and "real job" meant anything that was not self-employment.

Receiving the news from Jim was not the only time I considered, however briefly, flipping burgers—literally—or perhaps selling clothes at the mall or shelving books at the local Barnes & Noble. But the idea of returning to any real job and conforming to someone else's rules practically gave me hives. Besides, working twenty hours a week at low wages, minus taxes, would hardly bring in enough money to justify the time and energy lost to freelancing. I could make lots more with just one freelance assignment, if only I could keep work coming in.

Leaving my job in corporate public relations meant much more than simply exchanging one desk for another. First of all, instead of leaving me feeling like an impostor, my work now nourished my heart. You've probably seen those bumper stickers, "The worst day fishing/sailing/skiing is better than the best day at the office." For me, any day spent wrestling with how best to describe even the most mundane things—truck scales at highway truck stops, "Southwest Indiana Food Corn," a factory's material handling technology—was immensely more gratifying than an *hour* in any real job. I actually wrote about all those things, and the challenge of doing it well was deeply satisfying. In addition to supporting me, my work allowed me to be of service to my clients—a local jeweler, a tool and die maker, a bakery, and others.

At the same time, this commercial writing was only a means to a more important end: financial support while I established myself as a magazine writer. I wanted to write about topics that piqued my curiosity, let me have fun, or—best of all—could make a positive difference in the world. My articles and personal essays began to appear in regional and national publications, on topics such as learning how to meditate, microloans that allowed destitute women to lift themselves from poverty (one of these articles was reprinted in the *New Delhi Times*), and the lush fabric art of Penny Sisto, who lived in a cedar-log house to keep the moths away.

Freelancing liberated me from Byzantine office politics and petty workplace rules. It also challenged me in new, exhilarating ways. For the first time, I could choose my own work goals (say, having an article published in *The Christian Science Monitor*) versus having them imposed by a corporate entity (for example, ensuring that the people I managed processed an additional 500 claims a week). Being my own boss also meant freedom from supervision—fortunately, my self-discipline was up to the task— and from a schedule set by someone else. I could take an occasional extra-long lunch or a day or two off without having to ask permission—but only when work allowed. My firmest rule was "never miss a deadline," and I never did.

There were smaller joys, too. Never having to wear a suit or pantyhose unless I *really* wanted to. Being able to collaborate with Lynda. Watching through my apartment windows on frigid, snowy days while all those other people bundled in parkas and scarves slipped and slid to work, while I stayed cozy inside with a cup of hot tea and warm slippers.

The thought of taking another real job of any kind swamped me with despair.

I made it through that first lean time, even though all these years later, I don't remember how. I have since survived many other lean times. Checks arrived, new jobs came in, I counted pennies. I would be flush, and then not. Feast or famine—all freelancers know that story. One time, I produced $4,000 worth of articles for two new magazines, and they did not pay and did not pay, and then they folded. Another time, a national business-women's magazine assigned me a new article on microloans. The payment of $1,200 for 2,000 words was the largest fee for a single article I'd been offered to date. When the editor called, I managed to keep my voice calm and professional: "Oh, yes, I'd be happy to write that story for you. When do you need it?" And then when we hung up, I bounced up and down in my desk chair, chanting, "Twelve hundred dollars! Twelve hundred dollars!" and immediately called Lynda. A local business journal, which had long run my articles, hired me as editor, a part-time, work-at-home position that provided a small but regular income for several years (despite the occasional bounced paycheck). Sometimes I pulled a Tarot card during my morning meditation while asking for "today's message" as a way of guiding myself through the day. Recorded in one journal entry: "10/16 - Today's message: The Tower—explosion of old ways and a new way of life coming. (Later today—I had to buy a new car battery and 'X' magazine folded, owing me $1,300.)" A graph of all these financial ups and downs would resemble an electrocardiogram gone berserk.

Over the years, I dipped into my retirement fund several times—$2,000 or $5,000, for example—despite the penalties and extra taxes. Not the best financial strategy, but I could not bear the thought of taking another real job. Out of the blue in 1995, a utility company across the Ohio River in Kentucky offered me another writing position, as did a local ad agency, but returning to corporate life felt like doom, so I declined both and offered my services as a freelancer.

Along with hard work, I tried the metaphysical approach. In my meditations, I included affirmations for financial security, often saying them aloud: "I, Barbara, am always well-provided for by the Universe and live a life of abundance. I am a successful freelance writer writing for magazines and clients that pay well and on time. In return, I provide them with the best products and service of which I am capable. My work is respected and sought after by editors who contact me with interesting writing assignments." Or, nestled quietly in the corner of my couch—my favorite meditation place—I visualized three bushel baskets of money scattered around my apartment that automatically replenished themselves when I took money out, $20s and $50s burbling up like a steady fountain. According to the principles of feng shui (something I wrote about several times), I hung a faceted crystal in the Wealth section of my apartment.

Still, my anxiety revved every time it seemed funds *might* run short.

One night after several years of freelancing, a sound startled me out of a deep sleep. Perhaps it was a car racing down Lincoln Avenue right outside my apartment. But the jolt into wakefulness fired up a tape loop in my head, the one called "Financial Anxiety, Insomnia Version."

"Taxes are due again, and that means taking a big chunk out of savings," it hissed directly into the fear center of my brain.

"Sure, you save more now, but once you shell out those thousands, you'll have to start over. And what if some catastrophe happens in the meantime? What if your car breaks down—it's getting old—or what if you can't pay your medical insurance and have an accident or get really sick and can't work for months? What if your clients never pay? What if you don't get any more jobs? What if you're not a good writer after all, and no one wants your work again—ever?"

Wait. Stop. This was ridiculous.

I had chosen to be a freelance writer, and still chose it, despite all the insecurities. Another real job would only make me miserable again. But slogging down this mucky, fearful road over and over was exhausting and defeating. What was I going to do about it?

I took a few deep breaths and sat up against my faux brass headboard. Narrow, glowing ribbons of streetlight seeped in around the closed mini-blinds, and in the dresser mirror across the small room, I watched my dim reflection pull up the covers against the cool air. A little calmer, I tried to snatch one rational thought from the whirling nuttiness in my brain. And I found it.

I looked at the bed-headed woman in the mirror, and like one friend reassuring another, said quietly to her, "Barbara, you have enough money to pay your taxes. You have enough this time, just like you always have. You have enough for today."

Well, damn, I thought.

That one tiny shift in perception flipped my thoughts: My fear did not stem from any actual lack of funds at the moment, but from anticipating what *might* happen next week or next month. The fact was, even without piles of money, I always had enough for necessities, just when it was required, and often more. That had been true my whole life, all the way back to Daddy working in factories and, later, Mom's budgeting to continue paying the mortgage and to buy my glasses so I could see the blackboard and read my books.

I have enough money for today.

The tape loop in my head went silent.

I have enough money for today, and tomorrow will take care of itself.

The woman in the mirror and I scooted back down in bed, rearranged our pillows, and fell back to sleep.

Wish I could say all my money worries vanished that night, but I was still a freelancer with no other source of income but my writing. For years, my gut still tightened when I wrote necessary checks that gobbled up most of my bank balance. My journal was still riddled with notes like "got a $700 check today" or "paid another month's bills this week" as frequently as "no checks in the mailbox AGAIN" and "July 25 – I've made only around $9,300 so far this year."

Sometimes, I joked nervously about having to flip burgers, and one Christmas season, I even went so far as to apply for a part-time job at the local Barnes & Noble. Fortunately, I think the interviewer could see my heart wasn't in it, and he never called. Occasionally, my nighttime insight came back to me, and it helped for a time. Then I would forget it. Then I would remember, and forget again. Dislodging this fear was like digging up a hundred-year-old oak with a screwdriver.

Maybe I was just used to lugging around the fear and didn't know how to behave without its weight pressing on my shoulders. Perhaps my brain had become habituated to it—think of worry as nicotine—and I didn't work hard enough to release it. Or maybe the fear hung on simply because I was so responsible; someone able to blithely run up massive credit card debt, for instance, might not have been so bothered.

In nearly a decade of freelancing, until I remarried, there were many lean years, a few more prosperous, and perhaps two in which self-employment was more lucrative than my last corporate position.

But again and again, the most unexpected events rescued me.

A friend at the Chamber of Commerce encouraged me to bid on writing a few business profiles for an economic development book about Evansville—something for which my corporate and freelance PR writing had well-prepared me.

"I think they want to split up the profiles among several writers," she said when we met Downtown to discuss the project over lunch. "But they already know your work, so that could help."

I peered over my menu at her. "That would be great. And going to interview a few people would get me out of the house, too. Sometimes working at home is so isolating."

So I sent in my bid, hoping to snag at least five or six profiles.

Instead, the person in charge of the project chose me to write all the profiles—more than thirty—and that one job accounted for a third of that year's income.

An editor friend went to work at a Florida publisher and began assigning articles to me on everything from high-end fountain pens to the latest in computer technology used by the federal government. A decade later, the new editors still call with assignments.

One day, when my car desperately needed tires and my funds were riding on the rims, an envelope arrived from a non-profit spiritual center in Indianapolis. I believed in their mission and happily volunteered to write some of their newsletter articles. Walking up the stairs to my apartment while ripping open the envelope, I halted halfway up when I discovered the check for $250.

How wonderful, I thought. Thank you!

Back at my desk, I called the center's new director, who had become a friend.

"Peter, you sweetie. You didn't have to send this check."

"I wanted to surprise you," he said with a little laugh. "You've helped us so much with your writing."

"Thank you. It's a little miracle. It will pay for new tires and then some."

"You're very welcome."

After about ten years in Southern Indiana, an inner knowing in me, a soul itch, started to nudge its way to the surface. It felt as though some place other than Evansville, as yet unidentified, was calling to me. There was no urgency in the faint messages, so for several years, I simply acknowledged them, knowing more information would appear at the right time.

In August 1999, I decided to move to Tucson. Although "decided" might be too strong a word—there was no internal debate, no weighing of pros and cons. Upon waking one morning, I knew I was going. A few friends lived there, so it seemed a good choice.

On the surface, it was a harebrained scheme. Dear friends in Evansville loved and supported me, local businesses wanted my work, Mom and my sisters Jean and Joyce were only five hours north by car. Why would I give that up?

But just as my heart had pulled me into freelancing in 1994, it now tugged me to the desert. So I went, using more of my retirement money. Everything about the move fell smoothly into place. Even the national moving company, for which I'd written one of the profiles for the Chamber of Commerce book, gave me a 50 percent discount.

In 1987, I was hired as a corporate writer without any professional writing experience. Since 1994, I'd survived as a freelancer. Maybe my affirmations and bushel-basket money fountains had worked just enough. So why couldn't other miracles happen, too?

In terms of work and finances, Tucson was tough. My rent had nearly doubled from Evansville, and my 14-year-old Corolla finally gave up the ghost, adding a car payment to the monthly bills. With no business contacts, that part of my work was gone, and over the months, other work arrived only sporadically. Even worse, my financial reserves, never huge to begin with, were dwindling.

One morning after a near-sleepless night, I stood at the window, feeling shrunken under the old weight on my shoulders, heavier than ever. The desert vegetation, still exotic to my Midwestern eyes, distracted me for a few moments—black-barked mesquites, palo verde trees with skin and leaves the color of limes, prickly pear cacti like branching Mickey Mouse ears, multi-armed saguaros that grow nowhere beyond the Sonoran Desert. The craggy Catalina Mountains still took my breath away as they rose thousands of feet above the crowded valley floor. Indiana offered no sights like that.

Maybe I should go back there. Maybe moving away had been a mistake. Maybe no more miracles were coming.

Then movement overhead caught my eye. Their wide wings outstretched with grace and power, two coal-black ravens soared in languid spirals on invisible currents in the sapphire sky. Floating higher and higher, they appeared not to have a care in the world. Totally present in their gliding, fully in their element, they never questioned the support of the air as they lifted themselves in flight.

I turned from the window only when the ravens became dark pinpoints, still spiraling upward. For one more day, I could keep going. Today, I had enough.

CHAPTER SIX
What I Thought I Knew

"You get the love that you allow."
— Don Henley

Dang. I'd gotten myself into another dating pickle. I knew he was the guy, the one in the slightly too-large gray polyester dress pants held up by red suspenders, baby blue button-down shirt, and puffy, snow-white running shoes. He was coming across the parking lot to where I waited for him in the glass-walled vestibule of the Chinese buffet. He was average height and slender, except for the small pot belly that pushed out his pants a little in front. Heavy-rimmed glasses, as I recall. Before you think me totally shallow (I realize he could have been a fun, eccentric guy), know that there was something else about him that portended doom for the evening. I'd met enough guys through the personal ads to know when Mr. Not-Right was headed in my direction. Many of the men I'd met this way were sweet and pleasant, and we just didn't have any chemistry. But this one, there was no charm about him, nothing that sparkled or gave off any hint of lightness. He emanated a weird, too-intense vibe. I sighed. It would be rude to run off—besides, he could see me already—and I didn't have the courage to lie about who I was. So I decided to give this dinner my best shot, just to see if my first impression might not be wrong.

We introduced ourselves with a polite handshake at the door and then found a table. Before five minutes had passed, he asked, abruptly, "Do you believe in abortion?"

Geez. What was this? We had talked on the phone several times, and he sounded pleasant and funny. He had a PhD in philosophy. Certainly he was entitled to his opinion, but never had he mentioned this. I was firmly pro-choice, but that wasn't the answer he wanted to hear. Before I could reply, he continued.

"I just called off a friendship of twenty years, just like that," he said. I waited for him to snap his fingers, but he didn't. "My best friend. Twenty years. I finally decided I couldn't be friends with someone who believes in killing babies."

Oh, God.

"I don't think this is really appropriate for right now," I said.

"Why not?" He was ripping open little envelopes of sugar, stacked in neat bundles of three or four, dumping them into his iced tea, and stirring with a long-handled spoon. Rip. Dump. Stir. Before too long, the super-saturated tea could no longer dissolve the crystals, and they piled into a little sugar dune in the bottom of his glass. "Why shouldn't we talk about the important things first?"

I wondered if he always used this much sugar or if he was just nervous.

"All right," I said, resigned. "I'm pro-choice."

From here on, I don't remember much of our conversation. He was not thrilled with my belief, but he tried to overcome this obstacle and be pleasant. As did I, wanting only to salvage some dignity from the encounter and then escape.

We went through the buffet line, choosing among egg rolls and crab puffs, kung pao chicken and broccoli beef. On and off over the next half-hour, which seemed endless, he continued to grill me about my stand on reproductive rights. His badgering angered me, and a few times my throat tightened with the struggle to remain polite and my voice rose a little. I should have walked out but did not have the nerve to risk creating a scene.

We finished our fortune cookies, and I took out my wallet to pay for my dinner. He wouldn't hear of it. After a stop at the cashier, we walked out to the parking lot.

I practically trotted to my car, eager to get away from this tortured guy. Once there, I unlocked and opened the door, then stood behind it as I lowered the boom.

"I'm really sorry, but this won't work out. Thanks for dinner."

Quickly, I slid into my Corolla and pushed down the door lock. He looked stunned.

"How can you say that so soon?" he cried, with real anguish in his voice. "You don't even know me yet!"

Without looking at him, I shook my head and took off, half expecting him to throw himself across my windshield. I anxiously watched the rearview mirror all the way home, looking for his beat-up car behind me. But I never saw him again.

Now, more than a decade later, I don't remember his name. But when I recounted the evening to my friends, I christened him Fetus Man.

Until I met Ken when I was 49, there were other awful dates (although I remember none so terrible as Fetus Man) and so-so dates, thrilling dates and lovely dates. There were one-night stands during my mid-1970s post-divorce disco days, before AIDS made that kind of behavior too perilous and back when I believed any port in a storm was better than being alone and, just maybe, please, God, the one night could lead to More. There were even, I'm ashamed to say now, a few married men, including one during my first marriage. Between my divorce in 1977 (we would have divorced anyway) and meeting Ken in 2000, I lived with one man for a year and later with another for twice that long. Both times, in the ferment of my imagination, I leapt ahead to marriage, with zero encouragement from the men. Beyond these times, there were occasional brief relationships lasting from a few weeks to several months. Some were delicious and easy; most were a losing struggle from the beginning. Repeatedly I plunged in, ignoring the red flags flapping before my eyes and shutting down the voice in my head warning, This is a Big Mistake.

Once in a great while, a man came into my life through charming happenstance. In the early '80s in Sacramento, a cute, hunky repairman from Pacific Bell fixed my phone and, sensing my interest (OK, lust), called me later—after all, he'd had my number right there in front of him. Early on, he said, "I read a book or two in high school"—meaning he hadn't read one since—and I knew it would never last, but we had fun for a few months. A decade later in Indiana, a limo driver/bicycle repair guy with gorgeous eyes and a ponytail, a friend of a writer friend's friend, sat down at our table at a writer's workshop dinner. Great sex and conversation for several months, but neither was this meant to last.

Now and then, I met men through the personal ads. Most of these encounters went nowhere fast, lasting only as long as a drink or coffee, after which one or both of us beat a hasty exit. But among the first of these, in 1992, was a man who read voraciously and devoured books as quickly as I did, had such an elegant sense of style he should have been gay (and most definitely was not), and was almost unbearably handsome, with eyelashes and muscles like you wouldn't believe. He wrote me eloquent love notes: "I'm chiding myself for waking up and thinking about you first thing and continuing to do so as the day passes, rather than business and chores and myself alone—but what it is, is that you've awakened the lover in me." He was almost always sweet, even while drinking himself under the table. I considered going to Al-Anon to see if I could better handle his drinking, should our relationship continue. If only he got nasty or mean when he was drunk, I told someone, it would have been easier to break it off. After three months, I did break it off, with much sadness. When Lynda told me I was grieving "the potential, not the reality," she was right. I often fell for imagined potential—hell, I flung myself into the deep end of that pool far too often.

For more than two decades of my adult life, I lived alone, and mostly without any intimate connection—sexual or otherwise—with a man and the kind of love I imagined such a connection would bring. Thwarted in my desire to be loved passionately, neither was there anyone to whom I could extend my deepest love. Both sides of the equation chafed—not being cherished and having no one to cherish back. The hopeful times came for a week here, five months there, only once for a year and only a single time as long as two. Often for months and sometimes years at a stretch, I pined for connection and fell desolate when it was yanked away.

In one of the bleakest times, after my divorce and while living in Sacramento, I made a left turn while driving and incidentally made eye contact with a startlingly handsome driver going the opposite direction. With sparkling eyes looking directly into mine, he smiled so rapturously, so uninhibitedly, he appeared nearly bursting with joy at the sight of me. My breath caught at the intensity and intimacy of this stranger's expression, seeming as it did to be shooting out beams of love. Perhaps in the brevity of our encounter, he mistook me for someone he loved wildly. Maybe he was ecstatic about something totally unrelated to that moment. Maybe he was just a really happy guy. But in that instant, I was crushed: no man I knew smiled at me that way, as if nothing in the world could give him more joy than to see my face. This happened more than twenty-five years ago, and I still remember the location—Folsom Blvd. and 59th St., by the Corti Bros. market—as well the devastation that ripped through me. I yearned to be known in the way his smile seemed to know me, in the ways only the closest of lovers can know one another, over years and years and through all the blessings and catastrophes life throws at us.

Always, I was seeking this connection. Let any attractive man walk into the room, and my psychic radar commenced to running. Like the Martian on the old TV show *My Favorite Martian*, little antennae would emerge from my skull in the presence of any man to whom I felt the least attraction whatsoever—*beep*, maybe he's The One, *beep*. Three dates with the same guy, and in my head I was practically trying on veils and choosing the bouquet. Naturally, most of them backed off rather quickly; I sure did when pursued by someone I didn't care for.

Looking back through my journals from many of these years, I'm embarrassed to see the broken record of my neediness and desperation. Occasionally, there was a temporary upwelling of my spirits when a new, promising man appeared on the scene. But these bits are far outweighed by the pages of scribbled complaints and yearnings, which, except for the men's names, are all basically the same. There was so much more to my life than this: jobs, vacations, becoming a freelance writer, recording my short essays for the local NPR affiliate and standing up to read my poetry in public, several cross-country moves, delightful times with my friends and family, heartbreaking times with the deaths and serious illnesses of loved ones.

However, most of my emotional life was occupied with not having the one thing I most desired.

For years, I wondered what was wrong with me. I'm intelligent, creative, and attractive enough, I told my reflection in the mirror. I knew it was a psychological thing, a search for the father-love denied me, first by emotional rejection and then by death, the ultimate kiss-off. Therapists told me this could certainly be the case. And it could be the reason I most often chose men who were, in counseling jargon, emotionally unavailable and commitment-phobic: I was unconsciously replaying the first rejection over and over yet incapable of changing the outcome. That makes sense, said my rational self. I'll work on that.

And then I would stumble off into another emotional tempest with another unsuitable man, and fling myself into the primordial drama of trying to make him love me. I would phone too often, doing my best to sound breezy and fun instead of desperate to see him again, although certainly the desperation leaked through. Or I'd send a cute card (later email), thinking, "Surely he'll respond to this," but of course he didn't and then I would stew. Or I would sleep with him again, even though that was the last thing I should have done.

In retrospect, I'm able to see how all the melodrama at least catapulted me out of my normally humdrum existence to a place of intensity and passion, like being physically transported from the tundra to the rainforest. Although ultimately destructive to my well-being, the melodrama was energizing (and addictive, too), roiling my emotions to a keen pitch that left me feeling so much more *alive* than melancholy or boredom ever did. A psychic once reported that he saw me mired in "drama-trauma." Some psychic. As if I didn't know that. What I wanted to know was how to stop.

I wanted to be happy on my own. Really. I did. Well, if I

couldn't have a man, I did. Life would have been so much easier if I had been able to quell this yearning, or at least control it. People told me that if I quit looking for a partner, a good one would appear. Of course, those who said this were always married, often for years, so how could they know what it felt like to be on your own for decades? How would they know the way I felt during those special occasions when I couldn't even dig up a lousy date? Or all those parties I attended alone because I thought I should get out (and maybe meet someone!), even though all I wanted to do when I arrived was escape because struggling through chit-chat with strangers always made me miserable?

Year after year, there was no one to welcome me home after work, no one to share my meals or an intimate moment (or even an argument). No one with whom to build a life.

After my move to Tucson in 1999, I hoped the desert would prove more fruitful for love than my past homes. Once again, I turned to the personal ads, this time in the *Tucson Weekly*, the city's alternative newspaper. I met a few men, but my love life remained moribund. Why shouldn't it? As they say, "No matter where you go, there you are." My desperate patterns of relationship were as much a part of me as my bones, and about as flexible, apparently: I'll never have a good relationship with a loving man who actually wants to stay with me. I have to chase emotionally distant men, work to make them love me, and suffer when they don't. California, Georgia, Indiana, Arizona: These beliefs accompanied me wherever I went.

In late January 2000, about three months after the move, I was chatting one afternoon with a group of new women acquaintances, depressed and whining yet again about being lonely and man-less. I was sick of this—as I'm sure everyone else was—but wasn't able to stop. That's when Dee looked right at me and said,

"Maybe it's time to give up what you think you know."

Normally, these words would have flowed past me in the stream of conversation. Perhaps they would have held for a few moments, a twig in an eddy, only to float away. Or, I might have thought, Gee, she's right, and then ignored them anyway. Instead, by some accident of grace, they were delivered to me when my psyche was just permeable enough to allow them entry. The instant they hit the air, their Truth whacked me between the eyes, as in those goofy movies where someone hit on the head experiences instant amnesia. But instead of forgetting, I felt a clarity so piercing and lucent, my body *knew*. Down deep, a quiver of energy, a little earthquake, left me resonating like a bell. I had no words to describe what had happened. But Dee's one sentence triggered a tectonic slip that set in motion the gentle wave destined to change the landscape of my life.

Still to come was deciphering the mystery of what I thought I knew and how to give it up, not to mention actually doing it.

Early in the summer of 2000, an old friend and sometime lover floated back into my life, blasting to smithereens any ideas about changing my mind. He lived on the other side of the country, so our relationship was conducted mostly by email and phone, with a rare visit when he had business in Tucson. I threw myself into the Pit of Anguish once again over his lack of availability and desire to commit. I alternated between sending emails that wondered when we could get together again and others that said, "Forget it, I'm OK, I don't need you, let's just be friends." Once again, my journal pages were bursting with endless rumination about this man. I stapled copies of our emails in the journal and pored over them endlessly, analyzing what he said and my reactions, and his reactions to mine.

After several months, I finally ran out of gas. I slowed and then coasted to a full stop. I was done. This interminable pattern was stupid and counterproductive. I was sick of making myself miserable—yes, I was doing this to myself—over men who didn't want to be with me. I looked back to the emails from the old lover and now could see, time and again, where he wrote that he no longer wanted to be lovers with me, although we could be friends (coming from him, this was no rote gesture). But I had steamrollered right over that, still entangled in my beliefs about what our relationship had to be, all of which led me into more grief and drama. As I could see in blessed hindsight, his statements were firm and direct, but I wasn't listening.

Now I was on to something. Maybe this one string in the big tangled mess of my love life would lead me to the center. I pulled out my journal and, sitting in my Bentwood rocker in my sunny Tucson apartment, started to tease it out.

This had been my pattern with many other men, too, I wrote. It's not as if there were some cosmic plot designed to keep me single. Or that all the good men were married or gay (I'd never believed this anyway). Or that no men wanted to make a commitment any more. No. It wasn't the men. Painful truth be told, the only common denominator in all my failed relationships was *me*.

I took a breath or two to absorb this fact.

Then came the words that changed everything: *I don't have to do this to myself anymore.*

My hand stopped moving, having just liberated me from the most painful and confusing element of my life. I felt as if I might levitate out of the rocker and go floating outside over the bougainvillea, citrus trees, and the rare desert lawn of the apartment complex.

The simplicity of this insight stunned me. The shift that

had begun with Dee's words all those months ago had carried me to rest in this place: If I was to be happy, I could choose it, no matter my romantic status. It sounds silly to have had such an epiphany about something seemingly so basic, but there it was. Furthermore, I thought, given my relationship history, following up this understanding with action would probably mean being on my own for the rest of my life.

Now that I so starkly understood my own role in all my unhappiness, being unattached and happy became preferable to all the drama-trauma of the past. I didn't have to do that to myself any more. It's not as if this was new information, but it had lived only in my intellect. Until now, it hadn't yet traveled what my friend Jeanne calls "the thousand miles between my head and my heart."

The ultimate outcome was this: In choosing to be happy, I chose things that made me feel good and avoided things that didn't, even my own emotions. For instance, instead of moping around because I was spending another weekend alone, I decided to relish the time I had to read my books. Reading had always been one of my great pleasures anyway, so why not decide to enjoy it even more? I often went out to movies or dinner with women friends, so why not cherish their company as much as I would have a lover's? Instead of letting myself sink into melancholy when I saw a couple holding hands and mooning at one another, I mentally sent them good wishes and blessed their good fortune. I kept a gratitude journal for a time, giving thanks for my lovely apartment in its little oasis in the desert, for my ability to read and think, for my friends and my work, for the love I gave to my family and friends and the love they gave back to me.

Sadness still descended at times, but I didn't give into it as much. Using the advice of a long-ago therapist, when I truly felt a need for a good dose of self-pity, I let myself sink into it for, say, a half-hour and no more. Usually, I ended up laughing at my own self-created drama. And while my antennae still raised up occasionally for a look-see, I was no longer trying to lasso some guy into my orbit. I was content.

My head was not yet off the pillow that early November morning when the little disembodied voice began chattering: *Go get the* Tucson Weekly *and look at the personals.*

I mashed my head deeper into the pillow and responded aloud to the voice.

"Yeah. Right. Like that ever worked."

Go get the Weekly *and look at the personals.*

"Oh, shut up."

Go get the Weekly *and look at the personals.*

"No. Leave me alone. I'm not looking any more."

When the mental process we know as a thought originates in our heads, we can sense it internally. Cozily tucked within our skull (or so we experience it), a thought somehow mysteriously arises from the chemical and electrical functions of our brain, instigated by the mysteries of consciousness. We can feel it there, inside, somewhere north of our eyes. This particular command to get the *Tucson Weekly*, which had been delivered into my mental ear for several days now, was not a thought. I was neither thinking it nor imagining it. It was not an internal process. The insistent, disembodied voice was coming from elsewhere, sending its message as clearly as if it held its lips to my ear.

After several days, I relented, figuring my intuition (or my angel or whatever beneficent force it was) meant business.

In the issue of the *Tucson Weekly* for Nov. 9-15, I found Ken.

At the time, the paper's personals section carried a half-page interview with a single man or woman looking for a relationship. Called "Tucson's Most Wanted," it contained the person's photo. As Ken later told me, his friend Tish worked at the paper and convinced him to do the interview.

My intuition had great taste. The photo showed a man with mostly gray hair and beard, both neatly trimmed. His welcoming, engaging smile crinkled the corners of his eyes. I was definitely attracted. He had been in Tucson since 1978, had "two practice marriages," was divorced for 16 years. He was 54 and worked at IBM. In answer to the question, "Is there anything you would like to tell today's modern single woman?" he said this: "...women in my age group I run into appear desperate or so wounded, you can't get close or you smother or they hold you off. I need something in between. I've got wounds, so what? I don't live in it. I don't let it control me so that I can be available in a relationship—taking one day at a time."

That message came through loud and clear. It was an excellent reminder to leave my old patterns behind and create new ones.

Several days passed before I could work up enough courage to call Ken, even as I worked on strengthening my resolve to no longer subject myself to impossible relationships. Oddly, there was no phone number in the interview, so I called IBM and asked for him, praying that his voicemail would pick up.

"Willingham here," answered a pleasant male voice.

"Hi. My name is Barbara, and I saw your interview in the *Tucson Weekly*."

"Yeah. Hi. Thanks for calling."

We chatted for a few minutes, and then he gave me his home number so I could call him that evening. I did, and we made a date for our "meet and greet" that Saturday, at an art opening at a gallery on the east side of Tucson, after which we spent several hours over a glass of wine at a nearby restaurant. We clicked, chatting easily about how we lived our lives (he loved to read, too—a definite plus), our families and past relationships, and how we both tended to choose partners who tended to not be the best for us. We both admitted being tired of that and ready to change our patterns.

Ken said he wanted to talk to all the women who called as a result of the interview. No problem there. I felt hopeful, and unlike in the pre-Dee past, desperation did not overshadow the hope. If he wanted to be with me, fine; if not, fine, too. I had decided to consider this relationship, whether it lasted one evening or much longer, an experiment in self-transformation. Could I enjoy myself and let it bloom—or not—without plunging back into the swamp of neediness?

A week later, we went out again, and then again. Ken enjoyed chatting on the phone, and called me as often as I called him. By mid-December, a month after our first meeting, Ken had spoken with nearly thirty women and gone out with some of them. He called from work one morning to invite me to go out on New Year's Eve. I happily accepted, and then realized I hadn't had a New Year's date since 1988.

That evening, he called to say he wanted to date only *me*.

What unfamiliar territory: a man I cared about actually cared for me back. Ken was kind and generous, handsome and engaging. He did not run away; I did not have to connive to keep him interested. Instead, he was interested all on his own. We were cautious but equally smitten.

We went for a walk behind Ken's house one afternoon, stepping off the patio and through the small landscaped part of the yard into the open desert. Many of the lots in the new subdivision on Tucson's far east side were still unoccupied by humans, although it was a popular neighborhood for quail and road runners, rabbits, lizards, and rattlesnakes, not to mention the coyotes and javelina who often wandered through. An ancient sea had once covered this valley, and we strolled through the rocky sand left behind, dodging prickly pear and cholla cacti, and thorny desert trees like mesquite and palo verde. The Catalina Mountains ahead of us to the north loomed above the desert valley like sentinels. We were in shirtsleeves on this sunny day, basking in Tucson's typical Christmastime weather.

At the start of our walk, Ken took my hand and held it. We "bread and buttered" around a few cacti, our hands pulling apart and then joining up again. But then Ken did not reach for my hand and walked ahead, putting distance between us.

"Is something wrong?" I asked.

"I've been married twice, and neither of them worked out," he said, stopping to turn toward me. "Other relationships haven't either. We haven't known each other that long, but I'm afraid the same thing will happen with us."

"I know what you mean. I haven't exactly been lucky either."

We walked past the wooden skeleton of a house under construction. "Watch out for nails," Ken warned.

In my best philosophical mode, I offered, "Just because things in the past didn't work out doesn't mean they won't work out now."

Ken took my hand again and smiled. "You're right. I'm not going to worry."

Then he fell silent again as we trudged through the sand. A few minutes later, he started laughing. His eyes crinkled just the way they did in his *Tucson Weekly* photo.

"Now what's going on?" I was confused.

"I was getting all wrapped around the axle," he explained,

"thinking that if you move in, we'll have to remodel the closet in the master bedroom so all of our clothes can fit."

I laughed, too. "I suppose we'll work something out if that ever happens."

We celebrated New Year's Eve with some of Ken's friends. Later, he woke up next to me and said, "Love you. Take that."

"I love you, too," I whispered back, smiling big.

We snuggled and went back to sleep.

The next morning at breakfast, we caught each other's eye and burst out laughing: "We" were real, and we were in love. Later, in Ken's home office, he said, "Should you move in some day, you can have whatever part of this room suits you."

As a freelance writer, I worked at home. Having an actual office, instead of setting up shop in a corner of my living room, as had always been the case, would be a luxury. I was about to respond, when Ken turned away slightly.

A few seconds later, he said, "A big fear just came up for me."

"What is it?"

"We're getting so close, and I'm already afraid of losing you."

I took his hand and kissed it.

"Well, I'm not going anywhere, if that helps."

Later that afternoon, after I had gone home, he sent an email: "I'm filled with hope that a different type of life is possible after all. The time I spend with you fills me with happiness and anticipation of what may come our way. We gonna be havin' some good times ahead of us. I'll speak with you again tonight before lights out so I can entertain more lusty and fun thoughts of you for the rest of the night. You have my heart. Love, Ken."

I printed his note, held it to my heart for a second, and stapled it into my journal.

In my 30s, when I had lived with one man for a year and another for two, I nursed the hope—futilely as it turned out—that the arrangement would lead to marriage. This man loves me, I thought each time, and I love him. He wants to live with me, so he must be thinking about marriage.

Obviously, fooling myself had always been easy in matters of the heart. But as I approached 50, the idea of living together felt lukewarm and tentative. In response to my insight about no longer torturing myself with bad relationships, I chose to now honor what I most desired: a full partner in my life. Someone as willing to make that loving commitment to me as I was to him—a husband. My new, quiet sense of resolve bolstered my choice to live peacefully alone rather than subject myself to drama-trauma with someone unwilling to choose marriage. If the man did not want to marry me, I could leave and live with that, but I would not live with him. Never would I issue an ultimatum—"Marry me or else!" was hardly conducive to freely-given intimacy. Because my old, crazy-making way had hardly produced happiness, now I promised myself to choose a healthier, saner path that fulfilled me.

In our early conversations, Ken said he would like to be married again someday. Me, too, I said, and explained my idea of a "full partner." But over the months, he waffled. He loved me and often told me so. He said he was a better person with me, how good I was for him and to him. He even began investigating better options for his retirement funds "because I want you to be taken care of when we're old," he said, imitating a shaky, elderly voice. Such a caring thought! I laughed and hugged him. Yet he didn't know if he could be my husband.

We lived across town from one another. In sprawling Tucson, that meant more than twenty miles separated us. So I spent weekends at his east-side house, which was far more spacious than my small apartment. One Saturday afternoon, we were lounging in the Jacuzzi that sits in the corner of the master bath, wrapped on two sides by picture windows framing a breathtaking view of desert and mountains. Perhaps the emotional brew concocted of hot water and wine, swirled with the intimacy of nudity, drew us out, but some of our most sincere conversations happened there. "Want to take a bath?" had become our code for, "Let's talk."

"Why don't we live together for a year or so, and see what happens?" Ken asked, pushing aside a mound of bubbles. "If it works, then we can get married."

"No." I took a sip of Chardonnay and shook my head. "That would feel too much like a test. One wrong move, and I'd be out the door. Does that make sense?"

Ken turned his sad-eyed face to me.

"Yeah, it does. I do love you. I just don't trust myself to make a good decision about marriage any more. I blew it both times before. It hurt, and it was ugly. Living together seems to be the way to go for me."

I turned to look out the window and clenched my jaw to hold back tears. I wasn't anything like his previous wives, and he was a different person than when he married them. It could work now, if he would let it.

In the old days, I might have yelled at him, tears flowing. I might have stormed out and gone home, and then fearfully waited, wondering how he could be so cruel as to not call. Playing drama queen to the hilt, I would have phoned a girlfriend to get some sympathy, which would only fuel my sense of righteous anger. Instead, I continued to change what I thought I knew about relationships. Instead, I reminded myself: I don't have to do this to myself anymore. Even as my spirits fell to the pebbly bottom of the tub, the old desperation did not rise up.

"I love you, too," I said, intent on watching the floating bubbles. I wasn't sure all the necessary words could find their way out if I was looking at Ken. "But living together won't work for me. Before you came along, someone said that maybe I should give up what I thought I knew about relationships. That made so much sense. My old patterns certainly weren't working. In fact, they were hurting me and keeping me desperate and sad. Now I finally understand it's important to stay true to myself about the kind of commitment I want to give as well as receive, instead of caving in out of fear."

I took a slow breath and looked Ken full in the face. "You don't have to marry me."

Ken's eyes questioned that.

"Really, you don't," I reassured him. "I would never insist or try to pressure you. But some day, if you finally decide you truly don't want to get married, I probably won't stay around for long. It would hurt too much."

Ken reached his hand over to mine resting on the edge of the tub.

"Don't give up on me, okay?" he asked.

"I won't. But I'm a little sad."

"I know. Me, too."

In the side yard, a fat lizard lolled on a big rock warmed by the sun, and a pair of hummingbirds flitted among the few salvia blooms still hanging on in the desert winter.

"They look happy," I said.

"Yeah. I wonder what kind of lizard that is," replied Ken, willing to go along with my steering the conversation elsewhere.

That night I had a dream.

"I know you want to get married, so let's get married," said dream-Ken.

"No, that's so half-hearted," replied dream-me. "You have

to want it for yourself, too. I'm willing to give my whole heart to you, and I want your whole heart in return."

The dream left me with a question, which I asked Ken a few days later: If we never married, what was the point of our relationship? Being his girlfriend for the next twenty years—we would be in our 70s. How hopeless and silly that felt.

He had no answer to the question either, but neither of us was willing to give up just yet.

I was actually a little proud of myself. This standoff was different than my previous relationships. Or rather, *I* was different. In the past, I would have capitulated out of fear: He doesn't want to get married, so if I don't move in with him, I'll be alone again. True, Ken's reluctance saddened and sometimes angered me. But here was the crucial difference from the past: I understood that the only reason for my pain was my own impatience. Ken was not causing it; my feelings were my own choice. We were both doing our best to remain true to ourselves, behave with integrity, and treat each other with respect. I could not argue with that.

Our relationship delighted and satisfied me in many ways. I loved Ken with all my heart and knew he loved me. Despite his uncertainty about marriage, he never even hinted at breaking up. I could sense his interior wrestling match; his head was warning him against making another searing mistake, while his heart was tugging him ever closer to me. So over and over, I chose to enjoy what we had and not push the issue. Doing so would have turned me into one of those desperate, wounded women he had mentioned in his interview—the old Barbara had been one of them, and I didn't much like her either. That part of my life was over. Which doesn't mean that my old insecurities didn't surface occasionally. Instead of acting on them with Ken, I scribbled furiously in my journal, whining or venting as much as necessary, or called Lynda back in Evansville to talk them out. With time and enough compassion for myself, I knew I could replace my bad old habit with a more positive one.

After we had been dating just over a year, Ken called one night to say his fear of marriage was about him, not me. He even allowed that if he hadn't resolved it in the next few months, he would see a counselor to discuss it.

"Actually, I've stopped myself from proposing several times," he admitted. "I'm still too scared to do it."

My surprise blotted out any reply. But if we had been together instead of chatting by phone, Ken would have seen an astonished smile brighten my face.

"Barbara, you're too good to give up. Just give me time."

"You're a brave man, you know that, Sweetheart?" I said. "There aren't many men who could be so honest and introspective like this. Not many women either, I guess. Maybe we're both making progress on giving up our old patterns."

"Doesn't it feel good?"

It did.

For the second year, we had season tickets to the Arizona Theater Company. This season, we had chosen to attend Sunday matinees instead of a Friday or Saturday evening performance. Attending a good play was a pleasant way to spend a Sunday afternoon. In March 2002, the play was *Fully Committed*, a one-man show about a snooty restaurant. We were looking forward to it; the reviews had been good.

At Ken's house for the weekend as usual, I was standing behind the free-standing kitchen counter making us a quick lunch, a sandwich and soup. Feeling a little pressed for time, I wasn't paying much attention to Ken, who stood across from me, behind the opposite side of the counter.

"Hey," he said quietly.

"What?" I looked up.

"Will you marry me?"

Should it ever have happened at all, I had been envisioning a sweet proposal over a wonderful dinner out, like a romantic chick flick, perhaps with the ring specially hidden in the dessert (although that's *so* not Ken). Or maybe out on the patio as we cuddled on the glider chair and watched the desert sun sink below the Tucson skyline while a coyote or two scampered through the far back of the yard.

Now, I can't remember if I remained behind the counter or if I swooped around it before I answered. But I did say yes, and then wrapped my arms around my future husband, who looked a little stunned.

"You decided," I said.

"I did, and it scares the hell out of me."

"Not me. We're going to do great."

Several months after our engagement, just before I moved in with Ken, we painted the home office a striking yellow and blue. I'd be spending a good deal of my time there and wanted it to be a lively place.

Long before his proposal, I had mentioned how, were I ever to live in this house, I would need some color on the walls.

"You know, we would have to paint," I said, looking around the room as we sat on the couch.

His eyes narrowed. The interior was painted a shade of white called "Bisque," and he always insisted that its faint tinge of pink, which appeared only rarely when the light was just right, was plenty of color.

"Paint?" he said suspiciously. "Why would you want to do that?"

"Because I love *real* color and you love me and because this house is so sterile. You know, kind of like your life before you met me," I teased. "Besides, I've lived in apartments most of my adult life, and I have all these pent-up decorating urges."

He laughed. "Uh-oh."

"You'll love it. You watch."

"And if I don't, we'll just keep the door shut."

He loved it.

Next, before our wedding in March 2003, we painted the kitchen. I thought salmon would work well, but then at the paint store Ken discovered a shade called Nasturtium, a pinkish-brown he liked better. A rich color, it would enliven the whole room.

"You have great taste," I said when he showed me the paint chip, and meant it. "Are you giving up what you think you know about wall color?"

He shot me a dirty look and then grinned. "Looks that way."

Next, our bedroom became sage green and the master bath a deep rose.

One evening a few months after the wedding, we soaked in the tub. The setting sun glowed through the big windows, and the light reflecting from the rose on the walls washed the room in a delicate pink.

"It sure is pretty in here," Ken said, lounging in the hot water and looking around the room.

"It is. I love the light this time of day."

"I meant it's pretty with our paint job. The house looks great."

I smiled and raised my wine glass. "To giving up what we think we know."

My husband reached over and clinked his glass gently

against mine, saying, "I can go along with that. Cheers!"

He sipped his pinot noir, looking thoughtful.

"So, what should we paint next?" he asked.

CHAPTER SEVEN
Train Meditation

"...changing your mind is one of the best ways
of finding out whether or not you still have one."
—Taylor Mali, "Like Lilly Like Wilson"

In June 2001, Joe Zarantonello was leading another of his
Integral Journal weekends, this time in Tennessee, so I planned
a getaway from Arizona to attend the retreat. I looked forward to
Joe's spiritual wisdom and humor, plus the time to meditate,
read, and journal. It had been a hectic couple of months, and
some quiet time away would feel good. I'd miss Ken—we'd been
dating for six months—but he would be waiting for me when I
returned to Tucson. My favorite photo of us—me kissing his ear
and my arms around his waist as I sat behind him on his big
BMW touring bike—sat in my suitcase.

The Sonoran Desert that had been my home for the last
year and a half was gorgeous in a way new to me. The mountain
ranges curving around Tucson soar up from the valley to support
the wide blue bowl of Arizona sky, from where the sun shines
down more than 300 days every year. In the spring, the prickly,
thorny vegetation growing from rocky soil and sand sprouts
wondrous blossoms that could have been born in a far-away
solar system. On my drive from the Louisville airport to Pegram,
Tennessee, though, tears welled up in my eyes at the sight of this

environment most dear to me—magnificent trees that defined the skyline, grass and meadow, and even fields covered with spindly spring corn and soybean plants. The shades of verdant green that flourished with all the rain there—emerald and celadon, jade and pine—felt as nurturing as a grandmother's quilt. Only now did I realize how much I'd missed this lush setting that was so unlike the stark and angular earth-toned desert. Tucson was now my home—and a good one to which I'd happily return—but soft, green places would always tug at my deepest heart. Never would I change my mind about that.

Harmony Landing, the retreat center, was nestled on dozens of acres of lawn and woods, with wide paths for rambling. Not fancy but tranquil and cozy, it had rocking chairs and swings on the long covered porch, a sure sign of Southern hospitality. I quickly found a spot to covet there: a fabric swing hanging from the rafters, which cocooned me and swayed with the lightest push, turning me weightless as a dandelion puff. It was the perfect place to sink into a good book during our break times.

During the retreat, just as I had hoped, our days were peaceful yet laced with a good deal of laughter and the poetry of Rumi and Hafiz that Joe read to us. We wrote often in our journals, exploring the meanings of our lives. Our simple, tasty meals were spiced with great conversation. Joe woke up before every dawn and lit candles in the main room, where anyone could join him for meditation. The inner stillness I felt during those minutes matched the quiet peace outdoors, ruffled only by the morning greetings of waking birds.

A railroad track ran a few hundred feet from the retreat center. Several times every day, a freight train sped by as we were all gathered for the workshop, obliterating for a few moments any hope of dialogue and contemplation. First came the earth-shaking thrum of the giant locomotive upon the rails, ramping up in power and intensity as it approached. Then we drowned in sounds of train—monstrous rumbling, metal wheels screeching against metal tracks—that bore down on us like an army of tanks.

Unlike the distant train sounds of my childhood summers or the soothing clickety-clack of that Seattle-bound passenger train when I sat with my dad, the cacophony of this nearby freight train blasted my ears. It intruded into our woodsy retreat to fling me far beyond peace, all the way into anger.

But Joe Z. is a wise man. He smiled and called out loud enough for us to hear over the expanding din, "Train meditation."

Delighted at this new way of perceiving, I smiled back and nodded, as did other retreat-goers. No need to waste my energy on something I could not hope to alter. Instead, I could change my mind and accept it, even embrace it.

So I closed my eyes and sat quietly in meditation to welcome the train. The ground trembled slightly under the weight of many tens of tons roaring by, and that shimmy settled me down, as if calling back together all my atoms jostled apart by anger. The train's piercing whistle carried me inward, back toward the peace I rebuilt within the deafening motion of the rolling, swaying cars on their way to who-knows-where.

After that, during the times a train barreled past, we closed our eyes and sat quietly, wrapped in its weird symphony. With the physical act of willful listening, I invited the all-enveloping noise to embrace me back, and there I found my still point. I grew grateful for the grace of the trains' interruptions, for their encouragement to remain always in the present moment, always in my moment of choice.

Upon my return to the desert, Ken met me at the Tucson airport with kisses, hugs, and the surprise of a bouquet. On the drive to his house, I told him eagerly about finding the still point in the midst of chaos through Joe's notion of train meditation.

"Excellent idea," he agreed. "Probably the hardest part is remembering to do it."

I nodded. "I think you're right. Practice would help, though."

For a time I did practice, and Joe's advice helped me to find stillness often. During my morning meditations, for instance, it let me sink deeper and quiet my mind a little more. While driving in busy Tucson traffic, remembering the concept of train meditation kept me calm; getting angry because vehicles were traveling so slowly wouldn't deliver me to my destination any faster. On hectic days, stopping whatever I was doing and sitting silently for even a few moments helped me regain my equilibrium.

But on that future day, exactly nine months after our wedding, a screeching, monstrous train of events thundered into our lives and ripped away the effects of all my meditations. For months, I could find no stillness or peace anywhere.

CHAPTER EIGHT
Brain Wreck

There is a faith in loving fiercely
the one who is rightfully yours,
especially if you have
waited years and especially
if part of you never believed
you could deserve this
loved and beckoning hand
held out to you this way.

...

— David Whyte, "The Truelove"

The nurse left Ken's room. I watched her out in the ICU's central area for a few minutes, hoping she wouldn't be back for a while. I didn't want her to see what I was about to do.

My husband was finally asleep, his delirious thrashing temporarily eased, thanks to morphine and exhaustion. Someone had neatly stitched the Y-shaped cut above his left eyebrow. His blackened eyes were mostly swollen shut, and the bridge of his nose was broken. A heavy plastic cervical collar pushed his chin up and immobilized his neck. Now that aspiration pneumonia threatened his breathing, small tubes in his nose, or sometimes an oxygen mask, whooshed air into his lungs. The respirator's unwavering cadence meshed with the longer rhythm of the plastic cuffs around his calves, inflating and deflating to keep the blood circulating through his supine body and prevent clots. A horrendous bruise ran from the inside of his left elbow, down that arm and ribs and hip, all the way to his knee, where a wound the size of a quarter on his left knee dug almost to the bone. Brilliant blue tape secured a temporary cast around his right hand and lower arm, an eye-catching spot in the flat light of the pale room.

Then there was the biggest shock of all: His doctor had mentioned a brain injury, possibly a serious one, although we wouldn't know for sure until Ken was more alert.

I turned away from Ken to pull the camera from my satchel on the floor beneath one of the room's windows. As I stood up, the wide-open Arizona sky, blue as the tape on Ken's arm, filled my vision and helped me feel a little less claustrophobic in the tiny space. Here it was, the first day of 2004, and instead of welcoming the new year at home, we were in this room filled with beeping monitors, a few small chairs, and the bed with side rails, where my husband lay, covered by nothing more than a hospital gown draped over him and a light blanket, which he frequently kicked off.

He was quiet now, but yesterday he had become hysterical several times, once screaming, "Can't do! Can't do!" and thrashing in terror.

"Can't do what?" the nurse and I asked, stroking his arms and face to soothe him.

"Can't do!" he screamed again, hoarse. "Can't do anything!"

Was that how helpless he felt when he realized the accident was about to happen?

Later, he yelled over and over what sounded like, "D-O-A! D-O-A!"

Did he mean "dead on arrival?" The nurse and I did our best to comfort him as we wondered if he was reliving the collision in his delirium.

Now, with Ken asleep, I checked once more on the nurse's whereabouts and fiddled with the camera's controls. Then I stood back from the bed and quickly snapped four shots of Ken, ashamed of intruding on him while he was so defenseless but determined to have this record. I couldn't let him ride again, and these photos would be my ammunition.

•

Ken might not have started riding motorcycles again if I hadn't made an off-hand comment when we were first dating about three years earlier. He was 54 at the time, and despite his lifelong passion for riding, he had quit more than a decade before. The streets of Tucson were getting too busy and too dangerous for motorcyclists, he said. I blurted that I was a "repressed biker chick." How stupid of me. It was a joke, a reference to those sexy Harley women, tan in their spaghetti-strap tops, tight jeans, and boots, their long hair blowing free. It was the seductive illusion of the windblown freedom that appealed to me far more than riding itself. Were I ever to ride, I'd never go without a helmet and other protective gear.

But my comment was all the encouragement Ken needed to start riding again. He signed up for a motorcycle safety course to refresh his skills, bought a good used BMW touring bike—a beautiful blue machine weighing more than 500 pounds—and bought helmets, boots, gloves, and jackets first for himself, then for me. He began riding back and forth to work and elsewhere, once again exulting in his old love, which offered both freedom and the frequent opportunity to test and hone his skills

As intrigued as I was by riding, I was also reluctant to do it. Every week, the newspaper reported stories about motorcyclists killed and injured on Tucson streets, often because drivers didn't see them. Ken mentioned that nationwide studies showed the leading cause of accidents for bikers was inattentive drivers turning left in front of them.

"I'm very careful, you know that," Ken said, "and I rode for more than twenty years with no serious accidents."

I had to admit both of those things were true.

"You have to try it," he said. "You'll enjoy it. You're not trapped in a cage, like when you're in a car."

I loved him, and he loved riding. So I allowed his enthusiasm to persuade me. I worked up my courage and began going on rides, seated behind him on the comfortable rear seat of the Beemer. On Saturday or Sunday mornings, we'd head out to brunch in one of the little towns outside Tucson or sometimes just go for a spin on a gorgeous desert day. Even though I would much have preferred the car—where we didn't need the heavy full-face helmets, bulky jackets, boots, gloves, and earplugs—I enjoyed swooping through curves, inhaling the fragrance of pines drifting underneath my face shield, and feeling the air cool as we left the desert floor to head up into the mountains. Ken was right about the feeling of freedom. But to enjoy it, I had to block out visions of the two of us lying broken and bleeding on the pavement.

•

Ken's first accident, which we later named the "deer wreck," happened on June 25, 2002, a few months after he proposed and exactly one month after I moved in with him. He was riding home from work on the eastern outskirts of Tucson at a time later than usual on a road he didn't normally take. A deer standing on the other side of the road bounded out in front of a Ford Explorer, which flung the unfortunate doe directly in front of Ken's Suzuki as he was traveling at about 50 mph. While the front wheel halted immediately on impact, nothing else did. The back end of the bike flew up, Ken was flung into the air, and he tumbled and bounced for 200 feet down the asphalt, the 400-pound Suzuki sliding dangerously right behind him. Later, the off-duty Border Patrol agent driving behind said Ken clung to the handlebars as his feet flew straight up and over.

At home about two miles away, I was angry. Ken knew we had to get to the computer store before it closed, and he was late. My Mac had finally quit working that day, and I needed a new one pronto to meet all my writing commitments. The phone rang, and I almost didn't answer it because of the unfamiliar name on the caller ID.

It was Ken.

"Hi, Sweetie," he said. Something was wrong with his voice, but I didn't know what.

Upset with him, I was about to ask, "Where are you? You know we have to...," but Ken spoke first.

"I borrowed someone's phone. I just had an accident, and I wanted to tell you before some stranger called."

"What?" I was stunned. "How are you? Where are you?"

"Just over on Freeman Road, close to Broadway." He coughed.

"Did someone call the ambulance?"

"Yeah. The guy who's phone I'm using. Can you come?"

I arrived just as the paramedics did.

Ken looked so small and crumpled on the ground, his face smeared with dirt, his eyes alight with growing panic even as he cracked dumb jokes that everyone ignored. The paramedics drove the ambulance slowly so as not to cause Ken more pain. I followed, my car glued to its rear bumper.

Ken broke about a dozen ribs, some of which pierced and partially collapsed his lungs; he also cracked his pelvis. Later, we would find that his shoulder blade had also been fractured.

Then, in the ER, he died. Or at least it appeared that way to me.

When the ER personnel turned Ken on his side to take him off the backboard, he screamed in agony and fell unconscious. My disbelieving eyes flicked between his pain-contorted face and the monitor that showed his heart rate plummeting to 30, and then to nothing. To a blank, empty spot. The doctors yelled, "Ken! Ken!" into his ear and shook him. I stood only a few feet away, hands over my mouth, frozen in the knowledge that my fiancé had died in front of my eyes. But Ken's heart rallied, and the docs said he had only "bradied"—suffered bradycardia, or abnormally low heart rate—from the agonizing pain of all the broken ribs.

Already shivering in the cold ER, I was by then shaking nearly uncontrollably. A nurse came over and put her arm around my shoulders.

"He's going to be fine," she said. "We'll take good care of him."

They did, and he was. He was home a week later, using a wheelchair and then crutches while his pelvis healed and sleeping in a recliner because all the broken ribs would not allow him to lie flat in bed. I was happy to care for him.

Since my divorce in 1977, there had rarely been anyone else for whom I could care in any meaningful way. I had yearned for someone to love me and also longed to love someone back. With Ken recovering at home for six weeks, I could care for him and show my love in the most basic ways—helping him to shower or be comfortable in his recliner where he spent most of his time, taking his food to him on a tray, sitting and chatting in the middle of the day, taking him on jaunts to the mall just so he could get out of the house (and where he often rolled his wheelchair so fast I could hardly keep up—"I feel the need for speed," he joked). In this temporarily expanded role, I had a sweet and important purpose. It felt good, and Ken, who had been a bit of a loner for a long time, learned to let down some of his defenses. We grew closer.

Soon, Ken went back to work, and our normal life went on. He even continued to ride, something I railed and argued against. I was horrified that he would even consider it.

"You could have died," I said, extending my best argument. "And in the ER, I thought you had." (And how could you even think of doing that to me again? I thought but did not say.)

He was sorry for that, he said, but he would not permit anyone to make him feel guilty about riding, and he wouldn't stand for any fear-based strategies aimed at getting him to quit.

He was adamant. I chose to not argue any further and even went riding with him again before too long.

·

Ken's second accident, which we would come to call the "brain wreck," happened on December 29, 2003, the nine "monthiversary" of our wedding. We planned to cook a special dinner to celebrate. Around noon, Ken decided to run some errands on his new Ducati M900S, a model called the "Monster," the third bike that now shared the garage with our two cars. The lovely day almost tempted me to go along, but I had a freelance writing assignment to complete.

"I'll be back in a couple of hours," he said as he pulled his helmet on. I kissed him beneath the upturned face shield.

Around 3:30, as I sat working in our home office, little prickles of apprehension started shuffling through my awareness. Ken should have been home by now, or called—after the deer wreck, he always called to let me know if his plans had changed or if he'd be late. When there was still no Ken and no word at 6:00, I phoned the Tucson Police Department.

"Were there any motorcycle accidents this afternoon?" I asked the dispatcher, struggling to keep my voice steady. "My husband has been gone for hours now, and he would have called if he decided to stay out this long."

"I'm sorry," she replied in a practiced but kind voice. "We don't have that kind of information so soon. You should call the local hospitals."

She gave me the phone numbers. First on the list was University (of Arizona) Medical Center. A woman's voice there told me, yes, Ken had been brought in by ambulance hours before and was now in ICU with broken bones. She couldn't explain why no one had notified me, and she would provide no other information.

"You'll have to come down and talk with his doctors," she said.

A squeezing pain began to stomp around near my left collarbone, and my heart felt as if it would clamber up my throat.

"Can't you tell me anything? What bones are broken?"

"No, I'm sorry. I can't." She sounded as though she wanted to tell me but wasn't allowed to. "You'll have to come here."

I started shaking but squashed my panic into a little container somewhere inside me. Falling apart could come later. By now nearly in shock, I couldn't drive myself all the way across Tucson. I called Gary, Ken's best friend, for a ride to UMC.

At the hospital, the doctor ushered us into Ken's ICU room. My heart crumbled into pieces at the sight of my broken husband. He had a ventilator tube down his throat, and he was struggling in delirium as though trying to flee some horror. Steadying myself against the bed rail, I lightly stroked his forehead and said, "Hi, Sweetheart. I'm here, and Gary is, too."

Ken relaxed slightly and opened his swollen right eye as

far as he could, only a slit on the very outside corner. His brown eyeball skittered there, unable to focus or settle down. He seemed to know me. I hoped he did.

The sight of my husband in that bed, and knowing he had almost died again, summoned in me a resolve so deep it must have sprung from the center of the earth. I was now every mother bear who had ever raged to protect a vulnerable cub. I was fierce, my resolve steel itself. I would let *nothing* hurt him again.

So three days later, I took those covert photos of my wrecked, brain-damaged husband since it was likely he wouldn't remember any of this. He had to see what motorcycle riding had done to him. He couldn't take another accident. And neither could I.

•

The three-pound human brain is probably the most wondrous mechanism in the universe. It's also one of the most delicate, basically a lump of gelatin floating within the skull like the yolk inside an egg. Even though a human head propelled against a sheet of steel comes to an immediate stop, the brain continues its trajectory, smacking against the skull's hard, rough interior and then rebounding in a motion called *coup contrecoup*, damaging the fragile tissue and often killing uncountable neurons. If a person survives such an impact, it is with certain brain damage, ranging from a light concussion to a coma and even eventual death. In between those poles, many problems can arise, such as memory loss, impaired mental function, personality changes, and the inability to work or handle the tasks of daily living.

Ken joined the tribe of the brain-injured when a white sedan carelessly turned left in front of his Ducati that day. Having the right of way but unable to avoid the vehicle, he smashed into the passenger side near the back wheel. The sedan continued into the Super K-Mart parking lot as if nothing had happened and disappeared (it was never identified and the driver never found). Witnesses came immediately to Ken's aid, and an ambulance took him to University Medical Center.

After seeing the condition of Ken's face and, later, the blood-smeared face shield of his helmet, I was haunted by a mental image: helmet striking steel, face smashing into helmet, brain slamming into skull. His brain injury didn't show up on imaging scans—as is often the case—so there was nothing to do but wait and see how the damage revealed itself. However, it was likely that most of the damage was in the frontal lobes, which are associated with memory, impulse control, judgment, language, sexual behavior, problem solving, motor function, and planning and executing behavior.

In the first days after the accident, as his delirium and terror lessened, much of Ken's speech consisted of parroting words in a sing-song voice. Aspiration pneumonia made him cough, which frustrated him.

"Bummer," I said, stroking his forehead and smiling directly into his right eye, now a little more open, so he could see I was joking, trying to keep things light.

"Bummer, bummer, bummer," he sing-songed back, much as a toddler would.

Next, he began repeating nonsense phrases. The first was, "Happiness is, happiness is," in a gentle rhythm. I added, "Happiness is a warm puppy," which he chanted for a while and gradually transformed, first to "Happiness is a warm country," then to "Happiness is a warm dick." This he said while fingering his Foley-cathetered penis, a common behavior in male head-trauma patients, the nurses said.

As Ken's speech expanded, I grew more alarmed.

"I have to rewire your circuitry so I can manage you

better," he told me in all sincerity. After I showed him how to drum on a plastic basin, to see if he could hold a rhythm, he declared his staid, 77-year-old parents were members of a steel drum band—no, wait! A plastic drum band! He insisted he had to get up and care for his patients (he's a computer programmer) while Scott, our chiropractor, repaired his Ducati. He insisted it sat in our garage waiting to be ridden again, unable to understand it had been totaled and was in police impound as evidence of the hit-and-run accident in which he was the victim. He talked about imaginary people in the room with us. "They're right over there," he told me, exasperated I couldn't see them but still smiling vacantly as he usually did now. During his first night in rehab, when he couldn't even sit up without help, he somehow climbed over the bed rail, wandered down the hall and fell, hitting his head, fortunately without further injury. The nurse who called me around 1 a.m. said he kept repeating, "I have to find the motion. My wife and I have to find the motion." He didn't know where he was or what was happening. Even worse, he didn't know that he didn't know—a very bad sign.

He was transferred to a Vail bed, a canopied hospital bed surrounded by sides of nylon netting supported on a sturdy, padded metal frame. It can be zipped shut from the outside, so the patient cannot exit without help but has complete freedom of movement in the bed. The nurse said it was an excellent alternative to restraints.

Prior to this accident, Ken was one of the most determined people I knew. If he was able, he would push himself as hard as possible to recover as much as possible. The question was, how much recovery would his damaged brain allow? Would he come back all the way, or would he be unable to breach some boundary that would leave him a bewildered, diminished version of himself?

I had to face disturbing possibilities. Perhaps Ken wouldn't remember me or his kids, Phil and Kellie, or what he had for breakfast. He might remain unable to work or drive or even dress himself. With his impulse control disrupted, he might always gobble his food like a starving toddler, as he did now, leaving me terrified he would choke. And although present physically, he might never again be present mentally or emotionally in the vibrant way he had been before. If that occurred, what would happen to us? With no family nearby, I was his sole caregiver. I could end up our sole means of financial support. How would I cope?

•

The morning after the accident, I found myself literally walking in circles in the kitchen, pantry to stove to sink to pantry, and around again. After a near-sleepless night filled with terror and frantic calls to family and friends around the country, I *had* to eat breakfast before leaving for the hospital. My body required some sustenance to hold itself together so the little tremors fluttering all through me would not shake me apart. What did I want for breakfast? Toast? Eggs? Cereal and yogurt? I simply was incapable of choosing one over the other. All my concentration was focused on Ken: The invisible tether holding us together across the miles required my constant attention, lest he float loose and away, deserting me as he disappeared into a far corner of the sky. I called Marcia, our across-the-street neighbor and friend, who came over immediately and scrambled eggs, made toast, and offered support—whatever I needed, she said. Grateful, I ate what little my knotted stomach would accept.

For the next days and weeks, the unrelenting stress and uncertainty kept my adrenaline pumping, leaving me hyper-alert, as though a loud buzzer was always sounding throughout my body, as if I'd mainlined gallons of espresso. I slept raggedly for only a few hours each night, the phone near my pillow, ready to answer immediately if the hospital called. Each night before turning out the bedside light and each morning as soon as I awoke, I called the nurses' station for an update on Ken's condition. His nurses were unfailingly kind.

The pain that had begun knotting my chest when I first knew my husband was in the ICU had never abated. I did my best to ignore it. I'd had stress-induced heart palpitations—premature atrial contractions—before, so I knew it probably wasn't a heart attack. Besides, if I were sick, who would take care of Ken? Four days after the accident, the pain in my chest, grinding deep like a steel-toed boot, kept me slightly hunched, unable to stand up straight. Marcia made me promise to see the hospital's social worker—I had no idea that social workers were available to patients' families—and to get myself checked out.

So that afternoon, I kissed Ken on the forehead and said I'd be back soon, praying that was true. The nurses had told me he grew agitated when he couldn't see me nearby; he couldn't remember I'd just been there and had no idea I could return.

"Bye," he said, cheerful and distant-eyed. "Come back soon!"

I left Ken's room and found the hospital social worker to explain my plight. Gently and carefully, he listened and then escorted me to the ER on the first floor. A team of nurses and a cardiologist—wonderfully, all women—scooped me up into a nest of comfort while they efficiently ran tests. They empathized with me, an ailing wife with a brain-injured husband upstairs in critical care. For the first time since learning of the accident, I felt protected and safe. A dose of something delivered a few hours of the best sleep I'd had in days. The pain was not a heart attack, said the doctor, only premature atrial contractions resulting from severe anxiety, as I'd thought. She prescribed a beta blocker, an anti-anxiety drug, and a sleeping pill. When, in later days, the prescribed drugs did not relieve the pain or help me sleep well, I accepted the situation and let adrenaline, not sleep, fuel me.

The day after my ER visit, our friends Bill and Wanda arrived to stay with me. I could not have asked for better or more loving care: For the five days of their visit, they drove me back and forth to the hospital, to the police department, to check out rehabilitation centers for Ken—important activities that were far beyond my capabilities then. Wanda held me when I sobbed and one night even put me to bed when I finally fell apart. Other friends brought over meals and soup or invited me for dinner, but I was unable to eat much. Working was out of the question; fortunately, my editors understood when I begged off my few outstanding assignments.

Despite my exhaustion from sleeping only raggedly and waking most days before dawn, I could barely sit still long enough to read the paper over breakfast, my habit of decades. As with the food I could not eat, unending tension kept me from taking in the words on the page, too; they seemed to merely glance off my corneas. Always I felt compelled to *do something*. I ping-ponged among necessary tasks—talking with insurance agents, doing our finances (petrified I'd miss something because Ken had always done them), handling the paperwork for Ken's disability payments, emailing or calling family and friends with updates—and even then I could not stop, so I swept the floors or straightened up the house or scribbled in my journal and then scribbled some more.

In late morning, it was time to visit Ken. Hours later, after he ate dinner, I returned home and collapsed with weariness on the couch every night, surprised and grateful I'd been able to drive safely home.

Terrified by an ever-present fear that some other catastrophe would befall Ken while I was away from him, I felt calmer only in his presence, but calm only relative to the buzzing panic that never went away. Later a counselor told me I was probably suffering from secondary traumatic stress.

"That's a condition common among caregivers of those who have suffered severe trauma," she explained as I slumped in a chair in her small office. "It's nothing to blame yourself for. It's a natural response to emotionally overwhelming events."

•

On that day when my husband came close to dying and his brain was violently altered, I didn't know the National Institutes of Health considers traumatic brain injury to be "a disorder of major public health significance." Two million Americans sustain a TBI each year, leaving thousands with permanent disabilities. But in the weeks after December 29, as Ken was first in the hospital and then in rehab, I learned how unique a brain injury is among all the injuries a human being can sustain. Along with physical functions, the brain controls awareness, personality, temperament, intelligence, and cognitive processes like memory—all those things that commingle to form a "self." While our essential self does not reside in the brain, the brain is the part of us that animates it. A traumatic brain injury can kidnap the dear self of someone you love, dragging him far away as a riptide does a swimmer, sometimes beyond rescue, even though in physical reality he is holding your hand or smiling at you across the dinner table. I wanted more than anything to look inside Ken's brain, to see what the scanning machines could not, to find his lost self among the blasted neurons and bring him home. Instead, haunted by our present reality and murky visions of a shattered future, all I could do was wait and hope.

This accident was so different from the deer wreck; then,

Ken's injuries had been only broken bones. But now, having suffered a moderate to severe TBI, he was defenseless and utterly dependent. Worse, he didn't know it. That white sedan had crashed into our lives like a tornado, and now my resolve that no further harm come to Ken was unyielding, rooted in bedrock and bone. Through it coursed a sweeping tenderness for my lost husband, like nothing I'd ever felt before.

While some brain-injury patients become angry or violent, Ken was almost always happy, in a distant sort of way, a sweetly goofy little boy in a man's body. His therapists—occupational, physical, and speech—enjoyed him because of his cheerfulness and determination. Yet, although physically located in the room, he was not present; he existed in some inward place, unable at least for now to transcend the damage to his frontal lobes. He spoke animatedly but never really engaged with anyone, aiming his face at people as his gaze floated over their shoulders. He had no concept of time passing and no ability to anticipate the future. Without the normal mental anchors, he lived in the moment and simply reacted to events as they happened.

The staff and I frequently reminded him he had been in a serious accident and was now in a hospital, but he forgot. He knew I was his wife, or at least a familiar, comforting presence, but when he started calling me "Boo"—which he had never done before—I knew he had forgotten my name. So Kim, his speech therapist, hung signs in his room as memory aids: "I was in a motorcycle vs. car accident on December 29" and "My wife's name is Barbara." She also started a "memory book" for him, to which I added photos of our wedding, his kids, our house, and our cat, along with affirmations proclaiming good health and normal life. Ken recognized every acquaintance who came to visit and jabbered at them in weird and oddly chatty conversations (common with TBI), but minutes after their departure he had no recollection of the visit.

Sometimes, though, bewilderment and fear clouded his eyes. He seemed haunted by a sense that something terrible had happened to him, but in his impoverished mental state, understanding recent events was like catching the shadow of a wind-tossed feather. Several times, he cried.

"I'm so lost," he wailed, his face twisted in misery. "What's happening to me?"

I held his hand or stroked his hair and reminded him, again, that he had been injured but was getting better. He grew calm, a frightened toddler soothed after a bad dream.

One day, we had just returned from the rehab facility's gym, where he practiced tasks ordered by his physical therapist—walking on thick foam mats and around cones on the floor to help restore his balance, standing between parallel bars and doing leg exercises to strengthen weakened muscles, or using a beach ball to play catch with me or the therapist to improve coordination. After this, he usually needed to rest, so we had come back to his room until his next therapy session.

"Are you going to leave me?" he asked out of the blue, his voice aching with sadness. "I'm not the same man I was. And I don't know if I ever will be."

Commanding my tears not to fall, I looked down at my desolate husband, wearing rumpled pajamas and strapped into a wheelchair with a wide Velcro belt, the cervical collar still around his neck to protect a broken bone at the base of his skull, a post-surgical cast on his broken right hand. I hugged him and smiled.

"You're stuck with me, kid. It took me all those years to find you, and there's no way I'm leaving now."

He didn't smile back or banter as he once would have. Instead, he struggled inwardly with something that eluded him. Distress at this confusion twitched across his face. So I bent down and looked him right in the eye.

"I love you, Ken. I'm not leaving."

"That's good."

His face settled back into a blank calmness and his vision drifted past me, his current dilemma resolved and the memory of it quickly forgotten. He wheeled himself across the vinyl floor, and I helped him get into the Vail bed so he could nap.

My sweet husband. What would happen to him, and to us? Would he remain the same man I married or would the brain injury cause a drastic personality change? What if he decided he didn't love me any more? Could he eventually go back to work as a computer programmer, or to any job? His was by far the major income in our household.

Further complicating my thoughts and tugging at my heart was something he'd told me several times long before the accident: he would not want to live if disabled. Ken always pushed himself hard, and he hated being subpar even from a rare cold. What if he could not adjust to his new, post-accident self or make the accommodations necessary to adapt to his new brain-injured reality?

•

From the beginning, I helped with Ken's care as much as possible. I felt better being useful, and the nurses appreciated the extra hands. In ICU, when he was not able to get out of bed, I bathed him with warm, soapy water and a cloth, and talked with him and soothed him. Once he had been moved into less-critical care, he wasn't allowed to walk unaided—the brain injury had seriously affected his balance—so I helped my wobbly husband the few steps to the bathroom and stayed as the nurses ordered. The first time he sat on the toilet to pee, I stood a few feet in front of him, ready to steady him if he began to tilt, but he pulled me close and bent his head to my belly to steady himself. Looking down upon his balding head, I combed my fingers through his gray hair and held back the tears that clouded my eyes.

When he entered a rehabilitation center ten days post-accident, I spent every afternoon and evening there. We talked as he lay in the Vail bed, which was allowed to be unzipped as long as he had company. I read aloud to him, or read silently while he napped. We went together to his physical, speech, and occupational therapy sessions. I cheered him on, and sometimes joined in to help. One day in the rehab gym, he held me close as we slowly moved a few steps to a tune he hummed. When I helped him shower, he sighed with pleasure, and we laughed when my clothes got sprayed. When he was too tired to push himself in his wheelchair, I took over, taking him outside to the courtyard for some sun or back to his room from the gym after therapy.

In his first few weeks in rehab, Ken was assigned to "swallow group" for meals. This was a section of the dining hall set aside for patients in danger of choking on their food. With Ken's impulse control now haywire, he bolted big bites of food, hardly stopping long enough to chew before gulping another bite. I became a nag, perhaps too protective but terrified of further harm. I reminded him again and again to slow down, be careful. Stubbornly, he refused, brushing away my concern like a pesky fly. Once I cried in frustration, fearful that he would choke on huge forkfuls of dinner. He simply looked past me with distant eyes and continued bolting his food.

I allowed *nothing* to interrupt my daily visits with Ken, which usually lasted from late morning to 8 p.m. or so. From time to time, friends asked me to go to out and do something else for a while, take in a movie for instance.

"It will be good for you to take a break," they'd say.

"You look exhausted."

I was losing weight because I couldn't eat. I couldn't exercise because I was too tense. I couldn't work, couldn't sleep, couldn't meditate, couldn't do much of anything because I couldn't concentrate on anything but Ken. I couldn't stop talking about him when neighbors invited me for dinner, even though I tried to talk about anything else. Always, the tether of our connection tugged at me, terrorizing me with its fragility, the thought of how it could tear and carry my husband away forever. But if we were together, I could grab the end and hold on for dear life so no other horrible thing could happen to him.

"No. I'm fine," I replied to my friends, my resolve steely. "I have to be with Ken."

•

The day before his scheduled homecoming, Ken was rushed from rehab to Tucson Medical Center (TMC) with a pulmonary embolism, a blood clot in his lung that could break loose and stop his heart or cause a stroke. This life-threatening setback whipped my unending fear of impending calamity into overdrive. Already operating mostly on adrenaline-fed autopilot after a grueling month, I forced myself to keep going, one trembling foot in front of the other. Ken had no family in Tucson besides me, nor was I about to turn him over to someone else in any case.

The gray, depressing atmosphere of the hospital was crushing after the cheerful rehab center. Ken was not allowed out of bed for the first few days. Once the crisis was over, he received very little physical therapy, so I gladly helped him wobble down the halls when permitted. But after making such good progress in rehab, he was disheartened by the setback. He was weary of the terrible pain caused by the embolism—comparable to a long-lasting heart attack, we were told. The morphine helped a little, but the pain never left entirely, which wore Ken down. One of the drugs injected into the back of his hand burned his veins, often bringing him to tears. He was still wearing the hard plastic collar around his neck to protect the broken bone at the base of his skull, and it was never comfortable. His broken right hand was in a cast. Ken had always been physically active; now he could barely walk, and only with help. Worst of all, the brain injury had damaged his memory and other mental functions, which he knew in some fuzzy way but could not fully grasp. He felt thwarted and betrayed by his inability to function as vitally as he once had. "Will I ever get better and come home?" he asked.

One morning when I called, he whispered into the phone, "I don't know where I am. I think I've been kidnapped by foreign nationals."

I gasped. "Oh, Sweetie. No, you're safe. You're in the hospital. I'll be there soon."

He was regressing. He had to go back to the rehab center, *now*.

His doctor only made the situation worse. He would never deign to talk with me, but instead talked with only Ken—a brain-injured man currently on morphine who usually had no idea what day it was or what had happened an hour before. More than once, he told Ken, "Maybe you can go home today," when that was clearly not the case—any idiot paying attention could see that. Each time, Ken's spirits fell further.

When I arrived at his room one day, he mentioned how he had considered simply "floating out of here" the night before.

He wanted to die.

A cold, murky wave threatened to drown me. I worked hard to keep the shock off my face as my mind began churning with reasons why he should give up such thoughts.

Ken spoke again. "But I decided to stay because you need me."

"I *do* need you, Sweetheart," I replied, relief taking wing throughout my body and moistening my eyes. "I'm so glad you want to stay here. I need you, too."

"You come every day and sit with me and help me," Ken said. "I'd be so lost without you. I delight in your persistence."

I laughed at the unexpected formality of his language, which was so much like the old Ken, and he laughed, too.

His discouragement dispelled, he said, "I want to get through this and come out on the other side."

Later that afternoon, a member of his men's group came to visit. Ken told Larry and me he had decided to sell his motorcycles and give up riding. Larry was relieved, explaining how the group members had been preparing to do whatever was necessary to convince him to quit.

"If I'm going to get hurt again, it's not worth it," Ken said.

As relieved as I was, I was going to keep those photos in reserve. Just in case.

•

With the embolism dissolved after a week in TMC, Ken was transferred back to the rehab center for a few more days. He needed to regain the progress he had lost and be tested to see how well he could function outside the protected environment. Jeff, his occupational therapist, offered several choices for the test—tasks Ken would normally do at home—and Ken chose to make an omelet. Cooking our breakfast had always been his Sunday morning job, and he was eager to discover how well he would do. So Jeff purchased half-a-dozen eggs, an onion and mushrooms, and some shredded cheddar cheese.

On the appointed morning, Ken and I walked from his room to the patients' practice kitchen. He was out of his wheelchair, and I guided him to walk in a straight line; the brain injury still often sent him veering to the left. I'd brought our camera to document this momentous occasion.

Even though the kitchen was unfamiliar, Ken easily found all the proper utensils and equipment. Since his right hand was still in a splint—and he was not yet allowed to handle sharp objects in any case—I chopped the vegetables. Then Ken took over, concentrating but also laughing and joking as usual.

He broke all six eggs into a Pyrex measuring pitcher and mixed whites and yolks together, oiled the pan, sautéed the veggies before adding the eggs, then finally sprinkled on the cheddar before folding one half of the omelet over the other.

Only a month before, Ken had been unable to walk without assistance, read or figure out how to change the channels on the TV in his hospital room. Today, he had made a perfect omelet, gigantic and golden, on his own.

I snapped photos of the event. The last picture shows a proud, smiling Ken—wearing his red and white pajamas, with his now-shaggy gray hair and beard curling over his gray cervical collar, with a tan splint on his right hand—holding up his creation on a white plate. We took the omelet to the dining room and ate it for lunch. I couldn't have been prouder of him.

Later that afternoon, Ken couldn't remember the word "omelet." No matter, I thought—he had passed his test with flying colors.

•

Forty days after the accident, Ken came home. As happy as I was, terror still shrouded me, and in some ways it grew worse. Now I was the only person responsible for my husband's safety. Much later, a friend wondered why I didn't hire someone to help watch over him, but that thought never occurred to me. Even if it had, I wouldn't have acted on it: No one understood Ken or what had happened to him as well as I did, and no one would be as attentive to him.

His therapists had warned me about the perils of caring for him at home. Brain-injured people can be unpredictable and unreasonable. They might not understand how they're putting themselves in danger. They sometimes forget they can't do a task they used to do with ease, and then can hurt themselves.

Ken's balance was still off-kilter, and he stumbled a lot. What if he fell and hit his head on our concrete floors, or slipped in the shower? What if he stopped breathing beside me at night and I didn't hear? His short-term memory was damaged: what if he put something on the stove, forgot it, and burned down the house? He had agreed to not go out to his woodshop, but what if he did so anyway and cut off a finger or a hand? He promised he wouldn't drive, but what if he got behind the wheel anyway and hurt himself or someone else, or wrecked the car?

I had to remain vigilant. Ken still needed protection, and there was no one to protect him but me. Sure, he was slowly getting better, but full recovery, if that happened, was a long way off.

One morning shortly after the homecoming, I noticed that several large bruises darkened Ken's left side, which was bulging. He was taking blood thinners to prevent another blood clot, and we'd been warned that he could suffer internal bleeding. Panicked, I called our family doctor, who said to get Ken to the emergency room. Once again in full shrieking hyper-drive, with chest pain pounding and nearly faint with fear, I managed to drive Ken back to TMC. What if he was slowly bleeding to death internally? The blood thinners meant he couldn't have surgery. God, he couldn't die now.

Ten exhausting hours later—after I sobbed in front of Ken and a nurse, more from sheer exhaustion than anything—the "all clear" was delivered. There was no internal bleeding; the bruises were old, from injections he'd received as treatment for the blood clot. The doctor had no idea what caused the bulge in his side but knew it wasn't harmful (later, we discovered a nerve crushed in the accident had left the muscles flaccid).

Yes, we were relieved. But my skin had thinned to the sheerest fabric, worn nearly through by the unrelenting onslaught. I had only the most fragile hold on whatever was preventing me from crumbling into a pile of burned-out fragments.

But one more time, my resolve had seen me through. I had done my job of protecting Ken.

For weeks, I drove him to outpatient rehab sessions and doctor visits, sometimes two or three a day. Just scheduling and keeping track of everything felt overwhelming. Adrenaline kept gushing, though; my body was habituated to the buzz. Still not sleeping well, I was bone weary. It felt as if my life had revolved around Ken forever. I loved him, but now the tether felt so tightly wrapped around me, it was cutting off the circulation and leaving me numb.

One day Ken told me he'd been in the garage and climbed up on a small step stool to reach something high in a cabinet. I was furious.

"How could you do that without me there to help you?" I raged. "You could have fallen and hit your head again. You know how wobbly you are!"

"I was very careful," he explained in the irritatingly patient way he had begun to use, as if I was the brain-injured one. "I held on to the side of the cabinet and watched where I put my feet. I didn't fall."

"I don't care! Dammit, I've been watching out for you all this time, and I won't let you get hurt again."

"I won't get hurt again," he said, still calm. "I have to start doing things for myself if I'm ever going to come back all the way."

"Not yet. If something bad happens to you now, it will be my fault. I couldn't stand that."

"No it won't be your fault. If I think it's safe, I'm going to do it." He was adamant.

Still infuriated that he would not listen to reason, I turned away and left the room, angry tears falling down my face.

"I'm responsible for you, goddammit!" I flung over my shoulder.

•

As spring continued, Ken's improvement followed a stair-like pattern—a step up to remembering something for a lengthier time, better balance as long as he was rested, or a little less confusion in a stimulating environment like a mall, followed by a plateau as the gains consolidated before he took another step upward. Gradually, I began to relax my vigilance somewhat, probably as much from exhaustion as from seeing him improve. But even as the tether loosened just a bit, I remained aware and slightly on edge, one ear cocked to his movements around the house, for instance, while I worked in the office.

By early May, five months after the brain wreck, his outpatient speech/cognitive therapist, Susan Schuster, was enthusiastic about his progress. She appreciated his fierce deter-mination and drive to recover as much as possible; they worked hard during their sessions as she asked him to remember and repeat back to her groups of words she read aloud, or to decipher simple logic problems. I was proud of him, too. But I was with him all the time and could see that, in the nature of traumatic brain injury, even with the improvements, he still stumbled frequently, couldn't remember a conversation of twenty minutes earlier, or refused to accept that he could not yet do everything he used to do.

Then one day, Ken announced he was going to drive up and down our street. Before leaving rehab, he had signed a contract with the counselor assigned to him there that he would not drive or use his woodshop until he received informed medical permission to do so.

"No," I said. "You can't drive. You're not ready. And you signed your contract."

Keeping his word had always been a matter of honor and integrity for him, so I figured reminding him of the agreement would stop him. It didn't.

"I'll be careful. And it's a private street so I can't get arrested."

"Honey, that's beside the point, and it's not even true. You could hurt yourself or somebody else. You can't drive yet."

"I'll be careful."

"But if there's an accident, all someone has to know is that you had a brain injury and we'll get sued like crazy, even if it's not your fault." My voice was rising.

"I'm ready to drive."

"No!"

For once, I knew I was not overreacting and was prepared to hide the keys if necessary. Fortunately, Susan talked him out of this plan in a sensible way. I always seemed to get sucked into an argument with him, which his new obstinacy would never allow me to win.

"You've worked so hard, Ken," she said, "and if you start driving before you're ready and had an accident, that could undermine all the good progress you've made so far."

Fortunately, Ken agreed. Soon, though, as the coordinator of his outpatient care, Susan gave him permission to take a driving test with a special coach. This woman, herself in a wheelchair, was trained to judge the driving abilities of disabled people. Tired of being the family chauffeur after all this time, I was happy for Ken to take the test, although my anxiety fluttered in the background.

Just like his omelet-making test, he passed this one, too.

The first time he took the car out alone, memories of Dec. 29 flooded back: He'd gone out and hadn't come home for forty days. I was too jumpy to sit still for long. My ears stayed cocked towards the garage, listening for the door to roll up and his car to pull in. Our tether still tugged at me, but maybe a little less strongly than before.

Then before too long, Ken said he wanted to go back to work. My chest pain flared.

No. Not yet. We were managing just fine with his disability payments from Raytheon, his employer since Spring 2001, and I was working again. No. He should stay home for a while longer. Maybe take the summer and be sure. He still had that vague look sometimes, which meant he was feeling confused and lost. Too much stimulation—like several people talking at once, or being in a crowd—sent him reeling mentally and emotionally. He was still shaky on his feet, and stumbled a lot. He still needed to nap frequently; a healing brain steals a tremendous amount of energy from the body. He was driving again, but his reflexes were still a little slow, and heavy traffic sometimes confused him.

At our next appointment with Susan, she agreed with Ken about his return to work. As long as he started with only two hours a day, and his doctor and employer approved his return, she said, he could return to his job as a programmer.

She was right, Ken was right, but my emotions stormed. I had no words for the resistance that boiled up, but it was fierce, flowing from the same place as my resolution to protect him. Feeling like an idiot, I mumbled my excuses and went out into the hall, my jaws aching from holding back tears.

Sitting in the waiting area and turning my face from the people who walked past, I wondered why I was so afraid to let Ken step back into the world. He was a grown man yearning for his former independence and normal life; even talking about going back to work made his face light up. He was still fragile, but he'd been careful so far. Susan often declared he was one of her best patients because of his enthusiasm for pushing himself hard and never giving up. I knew he had to go back to work sometime. I very much wanted the quiet silence of the house during the day so I could write in peace again. In truth, I had been smothering him of late with my over-protectiveness. What the hell was my problem? Shouldn't I be overjoyed he wanted to go back to work?

•

Around this time, I found and copied into my journal a fragment of a poem by Rumi:

Go through the ear to the center
where sky is, where wind,
where silent knowing.

That is what I did about Ken's desire to return to work. All the terror and trauma of the last few months had pushed me into a state way beyond fatigue, near to craziness. If I was ever to recover—and allow Ken to recover—silent knowing was the only way to do it. So I did my best to remain as calm as possible, trusting that an answer would emerge.

Several days later, an insight washed over me as quietly as a ripple in a pond, and just as peacefully. After all the recent drama, it seemed anti-climatic, but it was exactly right. As I allowed it to unfold, it revealed several parts.

Ever since that evening when I'd received word of Ken's

accident, my life had converged to one absolute point. All else fell by the wayside as I remained laser-focused on my One Purpose: fierce guardianship of my sweet, broken beloved. I became the angel with the crossed, flaming swords blocking the entry of anything evil.

Never before had I felt so needed as I was by Ken these last months. As oppressive as it had become now, I had loved that feeling. My heart lifted and glowed to see his face light up whenever I walked into his room at the hospital and later at rehab. Even when he couldn't remember exactly who I was, he understood in his heart, if not in his damaged brain, that I was a stable, familiar presence who cared about him. I was his only constant in those horrible, terrifying days when everything, even his own Self, swirled in chaos around him. He was always so delighted with whatever I did for him, even the most mundane things, like helping him to dress, walking him to the bathroom, bathing him, or putting a straw into his can of soda at lunch when he couldn't manage even that. He told me he didn't let himself die because I needed him: He had needed me that much.

I did not want Ken to forever remain so dependent on me. If he had, our story would have been very different. But it was as though his dire need called forth from me a tenderness so inexpressibly loving and dear, I never wanted to stop feeling it. It pulled me so cleanly out of my usual self-absorption into the place where the best parts of me existed in service to another, who was wounded in body and soul. Long ago, I had chosen to remain childless, so perhaps this was how mothers felt about their fragile, innocent children.

In truth, the terror and tenderness of these five months had been so keen and piercing, had so stripped me of any frivolous distraction, I'd never felt so alive. But once Ken went back to work, all this would be lost. In allowing him to once again navigate his own way in the hostile world, I would have to return to whatever ill-defined, scattered things I had done before the brain wreck. My days of single-minded focus, in some ways the simplest and most meaningful time of my life as well as the most difficult, would be over. Gone also would be the noble drama of the strong, virtuous wife caring for her injured husband. Along with it, I had to admit, would go the attention I'd received for that.

All this drama had bound me with ropes fashioned of adrenaline and stress chemicals gushing through my system until I was no longer able to free myself, or even envision my life without the struggle. Dialing back the intensity to the level of regular life seemed so dull by comparison, so full of mundane struggle. Like being home alone to write in the quiet house all day, like waiting to hear from editors if they wanted a piece of writing, like not fearing what catastrophe would next befall my husband—like sweet, sometimes boring, normal life, like something to be cherished.

Against very high odds, my husband had not died. He was, in fact, recovering with very few of the horrendous effects that can arrive with brain injury. He was able to be independent again, for which we were both undeniably grateful. He still loved me.

And it was time for him to go back to work.

With approval from Susan, our family doctor, and the medical director at Raytheon, Ken began with two hours a day. He came home exhausted, sometimes afraid he would not be able to continue. But continue he did, working up to four hours, and then five, then six; by summer's end, he could work a full day. When he felt muddled, which was often at first, his co-workers were patient and kind. He dearly missed riding his motorcycles to work and elsewhere, but he sold them all to keep his word that he would not expose himself again to that kind of danger. The first brain injury meant that a second, no matter how minor, could lead to exponentially worse consequences.

For weeks, every time he left the house, the buzzing flooded my body, and the pain intruded lightly beneath my left collarbone, ready to stomp again if necessary. But once again, silent knowing provided comfort: there was nothing I could do to protect him out there, so the worry was only hurting me. I would simply have to trust he would remain safe and come home to me every day.

So far, nearly five years after the brain wreck, that's been true. Ken has returned nearly all the way to his old self—a miracle, given the severity of his brain injury—and I have recovered, too. Sometimes, it seems the accident never happened.

That summer when Ken returned to work, I showed him the photos I'd taken in ICU, first preparing him for the sight of himself so broken—of which he had no memory—and offering my reason for taking them. He studied them for several minutes and then raised his face to me, his eyes filmed with tears. He held out his hand, and I reached over to take it.

"Thank you for taking such good care of me, Boo," he whispered, using my new nickname and unable to speak louder. "I never would have made it without you."

CHAPTER NINE
Love is God

"I found God in myself and I loved Her, I loved Her fiercely."
— Ntozake Shange

White-haired Father Shea baptized me into the Roman Catholic faith shortly after my birth in November 1951. I've seen photos of tiny me in the long, white christening dress and bonnet, held by my mother standing next to my father, both of them proud and smiling, near the baptismal font in St. Mary's in East Chicago, Indiana. According to church doctrine, this ceremonial pouring of water on my head washed away my original sin, thus saving my immortal soul from the possibility of ending up in Limbo, which was not Hell or even Purgatory, but where my soul would never experience God, unlike in Heaven. Once so baptized, I was forever Catholic.

For a dozen years I wore a uniform to school—eight years at St. John Bosco, followed by high school at Bishop Noll Institute, run by the Christian Brothers. I tacked on my freshman year at St. Joseph's College because they awarded me a full scholarship. Our family went to Mass every Sunday and every holy day, such as Christmas, All Saints Day, and Easter. At Bosco, we began every school day with Mass, and after joining the choir in seventh grade because I loved to belt out hymns like "A Mighty Fortress is Our God," I often had to attend on Saturdays, too.

Even today, phrases from the old Latin mass ingrained through sheer repetition still sing in my memory's ear—*Kyrie Eleison, Christe Eleison; Dominus vobiscum, Et cum Spiritu tuo.* I remember also the feel of gritty palm ashes dabbed on my forehead on Ash Wednesdays by the priest who quickly muttered, "Remember, man, that thou art dust and unto dust thou shalt return," and, every February on the feast day of St. Blaise, how I raised my chin as the priest gently touched my throat with a pair of unlit white tapers bound by red ribbon into a wide V. This blessing was meant to protect me from respiratory illness and especially from choking on fish bones.

My earliest memory of church: Spring, mid-1950s. Hammond, Indiana. Maybe age four, I was too young to understand Mass but old enough to be quiet. This meant Mom didn't have to sit with me in the crying room at the back of our new parish, St. John Bosco, where parents watched through the big picture window and listened to Fr. Bart or one of the other priests through the speaker high on the wall. Unless I've transposed this memory with black-and-white family photos of the time, I was wearing a dark spring coat flared at the waist (Mom recalls it was navy), a white straw bonnet with a row of red fabric roses curved around the brim and white ribbons tied under my chin, and white anklets and Mary Janes. There was undoubtedly a frilly dress underneath the coat, but I have no memory of it now.

We were sitting near the front of the big church, maybe four or five pews back, my devout young parents with me between them. Without anything fun to do, I sat backwards on the kneeler, facing our pew, squirmy and bored. When I bent down and leaned my head sideways just a little, I could look underneath the pew and see trousered and nyloned legs growing from Sunday-best shoes that scuffed around like little animals (those were the days when everyone still dressed up for church). When the big people stood up, which they did often, I pretended they were trees growing tall really fast towards the high ceiling, and all the girl trees wore pretty hats. The swish of fabric sounded a little like the rustle of leaves on the trees in front of our house.

Shame and guilt: Now maybe nine or ten and with several years of Catholic school and the *Baltimore Catechism* under my belt, I tried to be a good girl. We were at Grandma's house on a Sunday or a holiday, and I read—my most favorite thing—as the friendly chaos of a big family gathering swirled around me. Grandma, Aunt Margaret, and Uncle Leonard, who all lived there, had the best magazines, like *Life* and *National Geographic.* Nearly every week, I brought home books from the library, but we didn't have magazines like these at home, so visiting Grandma meant I could read and look at the interesting pictures to my heart's content. I turned a page in *Life,* and there was a beautiful **painting**, with five dark-haired ladies holding hands and dancing in a circle. They looked so happy and free. Beneath their feet **was** green, and above that blue. I brought the picture close to **my eyes** and then moved it back, examining and admiring it. I smiled because looking at it made me happy, too. Then heat rushed up my neck to flame my face: The ladies were naked. It was a sin to look at naked people! Or at least I thought so.

Ashamed, I abruptly put down the magazine and went to the kitchen to get a ham sandwich with mustard or some of Aunt Margaret's nut roll, hoping no one would ask why my face was so red. I said nothing to anyone about my shame. Until confession the next Saturday, having this sin on my soul made me jittery, even though it was only a venial sin. The kind priest behind the grille told me I did nothing wrong in looking at the picture and did not give me any penance for it, although he did hand out several Hail Marys and Our Fathers for my other sins, like forgetting my morning or evening prayers and getting mad at my little sister, Jean.

Martyrs and priest: At home we had a book of stories about the early Christian martyrs. Fascinated and weirdly envious of their devotion, I read more than once about how, for love of Jesus, they welcomed their gruesome deaths at the hands of evil unbelievers who boiled them alive or hacked them to pieces with swords or shot them with many arrows. (Even St. Barbara, whom the Church in 1969 decided was not a saint after all, was tortured and beheaded by her own pagan father, who was then immediately struck and burned to a crisp by lightning. *That will show you*, I thought.) As the oldest child, I understood responsibility, so when Jean and our brother, Marty, and I played school, I was the teacher. When we played Mass, I was the priest. Girls couldn't be priests in real life, of course, but Marty was too little to take the job. We made the hosts out of Wonder Bread we flattened and cut into small circles with a glass from Kraft pimento cheese spread. At the appropriate moment, I placed the hosts on the tongues of my tiny congregation and then blessed them in the Latin I'd absorbed from thousands of Masses, raising my right hand in the sign of the cross over them: "*In nomine Patris, et Filii, et Spiritus Sancti. Amen.*"

Failed expectations: I always wrote JMJ at the center top of my homework or test papers, and drew a little cross beneath the M. In first grade, Sr. Leonilda, whom I loved, told us JesusMaryJoseph would bless our schoolwork if we remembered them this way. I still did this in my sixth grade class with Mrs. Crawford.

Pop quiz in geography: My palms sweated and JMJ smeared a little. A good and dutiful student, I normally did my homework faithfully, but one night I forgot to take my geography book home and didn't read the chapter on Brazil. I didn't know the major exports or the population, the rivers or the native language. I didn't know there would be a test. JesusMaryJoseph, I prayed, help me know the answers.

We exchanged papers with each other to check our answers: 67? My grade was 67? I flunked?

My only identity in school was the smart girl, the one with no real friends, the one who read all the time, the brain who wrecked the curve. I had nothing other than that. But now they would all know how stupid I really was.

Next test—no JMJ, no little cross. I knew I was on my own. Besides, if Jesus and his mother and human father couldn't do this one little favor for me, when I worked so hard to be good, then what was the use of remembering them on my papers?

Before long, though, my homework and test papers again carried this talisman. Although far less invested in believing its powers, I feared what would happen if I rejected JesusMaryJoseph this way.

Mad at John: I *loved* the Beatles. When they first came to the United States in 1964, I swooned over them, entranced by their cuteness and effervescence. Sharon Pennington and I walked the edges of the playground at recess, dreamy-eyed and singing some of their songs: *She loves you, yeah, yeah, yeah.* Or *Do you want to know a secret?*

But two years later when John claimed the Beatles were "bigger than Jesus," I was confused and hurt. At first, I was sure he'd been misquoted. But later I wondered how he could even think to compare himself and Paul and George and Ringo to God that way? How dare he!

Unlike thousands of people who burned their Beatles records, I still played my records and continued to love the Fab Four. John had said those words, not Paul, and Paul, the cutest Beatle, was always my favorite anyway.

My father's funeral: May 1966. Dressed in satiny black vestments, Fr. Bart, our pastor, walked around my father's casket in the wide middle aisle of St. John Bosco, swinging a censer that trailed a plume of fragrant smoke. He was followed by several altar boys in white cassocks. This incense was a symbol of the prayers we offered that day, which would rise up to heaven along with my dad. The smoke made my eyes itch. Oddly, this is all I remember about the funeral.

I quit: For my major teenage rebellion, I quit going to church. This would have been impossible had Daddy still been alive—I wouldn't have had the courage to buck him on this one. My decision required no great intellectual or theological leap. I did not systematically weigh pros and cons, nor consult anyone in authority. At age 19, there was only this reason: "I've been to church enough for a lifetime, Mom. Mass is boring, and besides, religion doesn't mean anything to me."

Mom's faith had always been the cornerstone of her life. She was heartbroken, and angry, too. She was probably afraid I would go to hell. But I was done with Catholicism, and for all I knew then, any religion. Between the fear of disappointing God and my parents and the fear of being sent to Hell, I'd had little choice about participating in the strict choreography of Catholicism, as though the Great Sheriff in the Sky was pointing a six-shooter at my soul while commanding, Dance!

For a while, having liberated my Sunday mornings was enough. But over time, much of what I had learned in the Church came to feel more like superstition or discrimination. Other teachings just plain didn't make sense. A wafer made of wheat flour became the body of Christ—not a representation of it, but his real body? The Pope—an old man who had forever rejected sex (theoretically anyway) and the love of a spouse—could forbid me to control my own fertility? And why weren't women allowed to be priests? Because a rabidly patriarchal culture of two thousand years ago had decreed so during their campaign to render women completely powerless? Or perhaps because misogynistic men later rewrote earlier versions of the New Testament in which Jesus endowed women of the infant church with more authority? If God loved us so much, why would he send us to Hell, even for the worst sins? Wasn't God supposed to be supremely loving? If He was, He would also be supremely forgiving. God as Supreme Micromanager was another concept I could not understand. Did God *really* care about whether I cursed or had sex outside of marriage or swerved from creaky, formulaic rules about how to worship him? Why would God meddle in our piddly lives, as people believed he did? Why would the omnipresent, omnipotent Supreme Being care about any one individual or treat his "children" like a father cruel to the one who ignored him yet dote on the toady?

Being an atheist: For two weeks during sophomore year in college, I smoked cigarettes. Thinking it would be cool, I held those burning cylinders between my slender fingers ever so elegantly, careful not to flick the ashes in the wrong place.

But I could not inhale the smoke. I would put my lips around the filter tip and breathe in, feeling the acrid smoke float back to the top of my throat, but it would go no further; I could not draw it into my lungs. My body was refusing (thankfully) to accept the unnatural behavior my mind was trying to impose on it. So, what was the point? I quit.

Around this same time, I tried on the idea of not believing in God. Becoming an atheist took some effort. Like smoking, it felt unnatural for me, steeped as I had been in the lives of the saints, church services, and catechism. While I could reason away my belief that God would punish or reward me, for instance, larger questions, such as how the universe had come into existence without a Creator of some sort, were stickier. Minus the idea of God, everything felt cold and dark. Eventually, I chose to believe that some kind of overarching Spirit existed, while leaving Its—definitely not His—form purposefully vague, imagining It as a kind of supportive yet mysterious presence rather than any kind of being.

My first wedding: In 1972, when John proposed as we sat in his blue Delta 88 parked in front of my house, he had already quit going to church, too. However, he had not told his parents, preferring to avoid the resulting mushroom cloud. Without question, our wedding had to take place in a Catholic church, so having to lie about our status as practicing Catholics seemed a small price to pay for keeping the peace with his parents. Tradition called for the ceremony to be held at the bride's parish, but since I was no longer a parishioner at Bosco, we could not have it there. John's parish, in nearby Whiting, was older and more cathedral-like, more romantic in that respect, and so we offered that reason to anyone who asked why we chose it.

We hit a little snag, however.

In order to be married in the Church, we had to attend three pre-Cana conferences (named after the wedding at Cana where Jesus turned water into wine). Led by a priest, these group sessions for engaged couples were a forum for discussion and exploration of the many aspects of marriage in general and Catholic marriage in particular. John and I barely made it through the first one.

Naturally, birth control was a topic, since Catholic teaching absolutely forbade it. I had already been on the pill for a year or so and had no desire to relinquish it. Even worse, according to Catholic doctrine, John and I had decided not to have children. Our plan was to keep our mouths shut until we made it through the wedding ceremony, although in our youthful arrogance, we were prepared to lie if necessary.

I remember the birth control conversation following these lines:

"In the eyes of Mother Church, the only legitimate reason for sexual relations is procreation," the young priest informed our group, most of whom, I wagered, had already flung that rule by the wayside. "So using birth control to purposely prevent conception is wrong."

John and I looked at each other and smiled. We had expected this. No problem.

Then the priest continued, saying, "Using birth control is a selfish act."

What a strange thing to say. John could not contain himself.

"How is that selfish?" he asked.

"If God wants to create a new life, it's selfish to deny Him that opportunity."

"That just doesn't make sense," replied John.

"It makes sense to God."

"How do you know?" John's voice had begun to rise in frustration.

"Because the teachings of the Church tell us."

"That's crazy."

Things went downhill from there.

As it turned out, the priest didn't seem to mind that we did not attend the remaining two sessions—he never mentioned that we hadn't shown up. He still allowed us to marry there.

My first look inward: Early '80s, Sacramento. I wanted to lose a few stubborn pounds. Actually, I wanted to stop lurching every evening like a zombie to the 7-Eleven four doors down and loading up with various combinations of bear claws, Häagen-Dazs, giant Hershey bars, apple fritters, or whatever other high-calorie sweets I couldn't seem to stop craving. I had heard that hypnosis might work and found a woman named Ellen to help me. Tall and kind, with poufy black hair and deep-set eyes, Ellen taught me the most incredible skill I had yet encountered and explained how to do it very easily at home. Lying on my bed, I slowed my breathing and counted back from ten to one, all the while imagining myself sinking deeper and deeper into the mattress or descending a flight of stairs. Sometimes, I could relax myself so deeply, I felt nearly incorporeal, with only slowed breath and a quietly beating heart to remind me I had a body.

Behind my closed eyelids, tiny flames sparkled in the blackness. Instead of shrinking my consciousness, this focusing inward carried me outward like billowing wood smoke on the breeze. By tuning into the silence within, I filled the universe. This was the most spiritual experience I'd ever had. My food cravings eased somewhat, but looking back, I realize that learning hypnosis, not normally considered a spiritual tool, led me towards an entirely new life of the spirit.

Thinking new thoughts: Around this same time, feeling lonely and missing a sense of spiritual connection, I began attending the big Unity church in town.

While I would never have returned to a Catholic church, Unity intrigued me. Based on the principles of New Thought and a metaphysical interpretation of Christianity, Unity rejects Christians' traditional obsession with sin, guilt, and control. Instead, Unity stresses the creative power of our thoughts, and when we take responsibility to choose life-affirming thoughts, we experience a more fulfilling and abundant life. In Unity, God is not any kind of being but an impersonal spirit or force that manifests as Perfect Love equally within every person, and living from that awareness is what transforms us. Also called Universal Mind, Spirit, Life, or Light, God does not reward or punish. Sin does not exist, only mistakes we make in ignorance of our true nature as Perfect Love, and we create our own heaven or hell through the state of our consciousness. New Thought does not worship Jesus but instead studies his life because he offers the perfect example for us to follow. He was not God but a man who fully realized his divine nature, which is something we all share and potentially can attain to the same level. Unity has no dogma and does not threaten or employ fear to maintain obedience. Unity respects and honors all other religions and spiritual paths. Rather than being mired in ancient times and beliefs, it continues to evolve within the spiritual implications of scientific and psychological discoveries.

Now more than ever, Catholicism felt as though it had been applied to me like a veneer, with fear as the glue. Unity's beliefs impressed me profoundly, more appealing than traditional Christianity had ever been. This philosophy introduced me to the warmth of a compassionate, more expansive spirituality that required no middle man through which to reach a God out there. Instead, I was part of God, part of Everything, and It spoke through my own heart. Unity services included a time of meditation, in which I eagerly participated and also began doing on my own. As with hypnosis, only more powerfully and with a more spiritual aspect, this listening within dissolved boundaries and took me, if only for short periods of time, into the Oneness, expanding me far beyond the cramped little box in which I normally existed.

But even with all this, I did not officially join Unity. Later, I even gave the Unitarian Universalists a shot, but their services felt more like a discussion group than a spiritual home. As a freelance writer in the mid-1990s, I began to write for *Science of Mind*, the magazine of the United Centers for Spiritual Living (formerly the United Church of Religious Science), another New Thought church, and agreed with many of its beliefs as well. Still I didn't join.

I'm not sure why. I've long preferred staying home on Sunday mornings with the paper and a cup of tea, and since my marriage, I'm not willing to leave Ken and his omelets or scrambled eggs and our cozy conversation. So maybe I'm lazy. Maybe being forced to attend Mass for most days of the week for years soured me on ever going to any kind of church on a regular basis. Maybe I'm wishy-washy, loathe to commit to any one spiritual tradition. Maybe it's that I don't like being ordered to do something out of fear of punishment; although that's not part of New Thought, it was certainly true with Catholicism. I'm typically not a joiner of groups, so perhaps that's what keeps me outside the church doors.

I also cannot forget that religion is responsible for so many terrible things in this world, even today: Muslim women beaten in the street for inadvertently showing a strand of hair or an ankle, or sentenced to a hundred lashes because they were raped; a president who flaunts his Christianity, even says God speaks to him, but who takes his country into war based on falsehoods; men who fly airliners into skyscrapers and others who execute families because they belong to the "wrong" sect; or Christians in positions of authority who use their religious beliefs as a club against others yet are themselves involved in whatever they so high-and-mightily oppose—drug abuse, infidelity, gay sex.

Yes, there are many truly good people who are religious and appalled at these fundamentalist extremes. I admire them and applaud their efforts. However, adhering to a religious faith is not a prerequisite for being an ethical and moral person, and their way is not my way.

Connection: Evansville, spring, mid-1990s. In the midst of an afternoon walk I gloried in the pushy exuberance of the life busting out all around me. Everything seemed to have an exclamation point embedded in it: Azaleas! Daffodils! Leaves! Grass! Sunlight! On this day, I found myself wondering how to explain God to my daughter, had she ever existed. I had no idea why it suddenly felt crucial to have this explanation. But even as the question floated into my consciousness, the answer arrived. It was not exactly a vision, because I did not see it as much as feel it. Suddenly, everything around me was vibrating with energy— or rather, its true nature, being nothing but energy, revealed itself. All the little energy fields that manifested as flowers and trees and shrubs, even the jogger across the street, vibrated and rippled outward, finally blending into all the others until no separation existed.

This numinous experience of only a few moments buoyed me for days. I felt blessed and joined to the entire universe, that amazing, intricate web of connections in which everything co-exists. Looking at my lunch one day soon afterward, it was as if

I'd never seen soup before. Not the reality of soup, anyway, which went far beyond this tasty stuff in the bowl before me. The reality of this meal was sunlight and rain combined with the labor of hundreds of people who had raised up the chicken, rice, and bright moons of carrot from the earth and turned them into a nutritious meal that would sustain me, only to return to the earth when I did, in a perfect, eternal transfer of energy.

Honoring the Goddess: In July 1998, I spent a night in San Francisco's Grace Cathedral. The vast sacred space embraced me as I entered that evening, and my heart expanded outward in greeting. In the junction where that sacred tenderness met my heart's longing, the peace reached so deep, I nearly cried.

Lugging sleeping bags, about a hundred women had come here to honor the Goddess in the annual Women's Dream Quest. For me, this overnight stay was an opportunity to do something the patriarchal Catholic Church would never have condoned: to honor my own sacred nature as a woman, and that of all women, by honoring the Divine Feminine as expressed in the figures of age-old goddesses.

Gray stone pillars held up the vaulted ceiling rising more than 100 feet above the floor, dwarfing the women milling below. Even with lights blazing, the huge interior was dim, the central brightness fading away towards the farthest corners. Wide lengths of fabric, perhaps thirty or more feet long, hung in graceful swoops above our heads; the bright pink and yellow billows pulled our attention upward like clouds, bearing the sunset inside the massive Gothic-like structure. At the back, behind rows of pews, a 40-foot tapestry labyrinth covered a section of the stone floor.

I had been studying and writing about labyrinths, so having the opportunity to walk the one in Grace Cathedral, a progressive Episcopal church, lured me from Indiana to San Francisco. This indoor labyrinth, like the stone one embedded outside in the courtyard, was a copy of the one medieval craftsmen had built into the floor of Chartres Cathedral, which had been a sacred destination for Christian pilgrims of the time. Yet labyrinths, which are based on principles of sacred geometry, existed a thousand years before Christianity and now are thought by some to be an archetype of the feminine on which walkers spiral inward along the directed path and then out again, reborn.

We all walked the labyrinth, either barefoot or wearing socks. The retreat leaders explained that we could set an intention before we entered the circling path and hold it in our hearts until we reached the center, where we might pause for a few minutes in contemplation before turning outward again. Nearly a decade later, I no longer remember my intention, just that my walk deepened the peace that had embraced me earlier.

During the celebration, we sang along with the chant "Ancient Mother" by Robert Gass— "Ancient Mother, I hear you calling. Ancient Mother, I hear your song"—as we unrolled a long, thin scroll bearing the names of ancient goddesses sung by the chorus behind the main chant—Isis, Astarte, Pele, Artemis, Kali, Shakti, Maya, Shekina, Sophia, and others. Never once during my days as a Catholic had I felt so moved in a spiritual ceremony, and given the tears glistening in many eyes, other women were equally touched.

Later, when we broke up into small discussion groups, our group leader offered some female-centered cards from which we could choose one. Immediately, I spotted mine and claimed it. Flipping it over, I saw the title, "Dance (first version)" by Henri Matisse: a circle of five nude women holding hands and dancing. Finally, I knew the name of the painting that had caused me such shame forty years earlier. But now, I celebrated it and later hung it near my desk for a time.

When our celebration ended, we slept in the cathedral, in small groups gathered in alcoves along the walls or individually in the pews. Despite the stone floor, I slept soundly and awoke refreshed a little after 4:00 in the hushed, darkened church. Alone and in my stocking feet, I walked the labyrinth, rendered in wool and soft underfoot, while the other women slept. The sounds of their quiet breathing rose up and rippled outward, the breath of the sleeping Goddess filling the immense church.

The ceremony and my prayerful walks along the labyrinth further opened me to the creative feminine spirit that exists throughout the universe, but which most religions deny or call blasphemy. For one night in this massive Christian church fashioned of stone, the Goddess reigned. In this event that was deeply spiritual but not in the least religious, I felt more whole and honored than I ever had in the Catholic church.

God is Everywhere: Somewhere along the way, I started reading about quantum physics, the study of energy at its most foundational level, far below the level of atoms, which are gigantic in comparison to the bits of energy that make up the universe. *Nothing exists but this energy.* We just happen to experience it as numerous forms and manifestations: the maple beginning to turn scarlet outside the office window, the black cat dappled golden with sunlight asleep on the desk, or twinkling Orion far overhead in the night sky. All of these are made of energy, as is every other particle of the universe. We may believe the cat on the desk to be a solid object, particularly when he tries to bite our outstretched hand, but in fact if we could look deeply enough, we would find he is nothing but energy, as are we. Furthermore, say the quantum experts, this energy exists only as potential until something causes it to take on a form we're able to perceive.

Certainly, I'm no more a quantum physicist than Einstein was bald. So my understanding of all this is elementary, at best. Yet the more I learn about the quantum world, the more possible an idea seems to me. This is how it goes.

Thanks to the *Baltimore Catechism*, I learned in first grade that God is everywhere. But I also knew then that God actually lived far up in the sky, in Heaven. So in blending those conflicting images, God became for me a kind of invisible giant, big as the sky, with magic eyes that could see everything everywhere. (Thankfully, I never had any creepy thoughts about this, like God watching me in the bathroom.) I grew up and properly left behind my childish image of God as the Watching Giant. Much later, I learned about New Thought's philosophy that God is a principle of Perfect Love within everyone. That made sense to me, more than mortal sin, damnation, and forbidden birth control. Even so, my intellect continued to hold God at arm's length; God was still somewhere outside of me.

Just recently, I was walking through the house with an armload of laundry, not pondering the holy mysteries in the least, when grace descended upon me or perhaps, less poetically, all the right neurons and synapses clicked into place in my brain. Whatever the cause, that old separation dissolved in an instant. A thought simply telegraphed itself into my heart, its beauty filling me to the brim: How could God be everywhere, in every little nook and cranny, every atom and quark of the universe, and not be in me? If God is *every*where, and I am in that everywhere, I am part of God, or Source or Spirit or whatever name I choose to call It.

Finally, this notion coalesced for me, and I understood in head, heart, and spirit. It inspires and engages me far more than any commandment, precept, or rule of Catholicism. It removes separation, judgment, and walls, just as I experienced that spring day during my walk.

As I am part of God, so are you, as is everyone and everything. From Mother Teresa and the Dalai Lama to Osama bin Laden and Hitler, from the most wretched refugee to billionaires in their lives of luxury, from a bacteria to a sequoia to the largest galaxy in the universe—in fact, the entire universe itself—all are part of Perfect Love. (Yes, I also have extreme difficulty including mass murderers and champions of genocide here. The reason why I have: On the physical plane, some souls have rejected Love and chosen to allow brutality to replace every iota of empathy for others' suffering and any semblance of humanity. Yet, even as we must hold them accountable—while doing our best to apply justice as well as compassion, in the Ultimate Reality, there is no separation from the One.)

In the scientific view, nothing exists except energy. In my eclectic spiritual view, much as New Thought teaches, nothing exists except Perfect Love. If we all acted in light of that (admittedly, usually an extremely difficult thing to do) and understood how we are inextricably woven into a Loving Wholeness, we would not need threats and fear to keep us in line. Instead, we would act honorably and lovingly simply because that's *who we really are*. Yes, I understand this sounds simplistic and naïve. But in the end, it feels to me both more challenging and more worthwhile to act from the personal responsibility of loving one another than to act out of fear of punishment from some outside entity hurling thunderbolts or threatening hellfire. Furthermore, isn't this business of loving one another what Jesus taught, minus all the misogynistic, political, made-up rules piled on over the centuries?

Where I now rest: I recently interviewed writer Kate Braestrup, who is also a Unitarian Universalist minister and a chaplain with the Maine State Warden Service, the law enforcement branch responsible for patrolling Maine's state parks. I asked her about her definition of God. As so often happens for me, the synchronicity of finding this definition and pondering spirituality for myself occurred at the perfect time.

As Kate describes in her memoir, *Here if You Need Me*, a major part of her job as chaplain is to wait with families and offer support and comfort while the wardens search the forest for a lost child or retrieve the body of a loved one from a frozen lake or the base of a wilderness cliff. She suffered a similar horror when her husband, Maine State Trooper Drew Griffith, was killed in a car accident. In those terrible days after Drew's death, she says, her definition of God became the overwhelming love, care, and compassion she received. Today, when someone asks her where God was during a tragedy, she replies with what she knows is true for her: "I take that Scripture very seriously, that God is love. Love doesn't smash trucks into one another, love doesn't break the ice under people. But love does show up when something awful happens. Love is there to comfort you, and any way that love arrives, that's where God is."

In all my spiritual wanderings, never have I encountered any better definition of God than this. My soul's task, then, is to offer love as best I can. Sometimes, perhaps most times, it will be imperfect and shaky. Sometimes I will not be able to offer it at all for petty or foolish reasons, although I will work to see that does not happen often. Every day, I have opportunities to extend love to someone. I can be respectful to the telemarketer who calls during dinner instead of banging down the phone in his ear. I can listen patiently to a suffering friend or family member instead of watching the clock because I think I have too much else to do. I can understand how my husband did his best to remember an occasion special to me but was let down by his damaged memory. I can smile at the beleaguered clerk, or hold the door open for the shopper behind me, even if he's yakking into his cell phone and whisking past me as if he owns the place. Most of all, I can do my best to be compassionate and to forgive transgressions, knowing that we all bear heavy burdens.

Every day, there are thousands of ways, large and small, in which we can extend love to one another. The most difficult part is often arriving at the understanding that we can choose to do so.

Having found in Kate's words my spiritual truth so perfectly expressed, I can take an easy way out of this essay. As a human being, though, living this way is the hardest thing I can ever hope to do. Yet it is the way that will bring me closest to the God I choose to believe is Everywhere.

CHAPTER TEN
Two Snakes

Tucson, Spring 2007

The physical labor felt good. Bending and lifting, stretching and carrying restored me to good humor and got my blood flowing again. This particular Tuesday, I'd been inside all day, hunched over my desk, researching and writing a complicated article. Ken had gone out to a late afternoon movie and dinner, so it was up to me to collect the trash from wastebaskets around the house and get the garbage and recycle barrels to the end of our driveway for pickup the next morning. The bulging white trash bag went into the regulation City of Tucson green barrel, while the recyclables went into the blue one. I pushed my sandaled foot against the bottom edge of the trash barrel to tilt it backwards onto its two black wheels and lugged it to the edge of the street. Then I did the same with the recycle barrel.

The late afternoon air was balmy, typical for a spring day in the desert. The evening would be pleasurably cool. I stood there for a few minutes, absorbing the still-wondrous site of the Catalina and Rincon mountains rimming the north-to-east curve of the valley. The light was just beginning to melt into its evening gold, glazing the brown and green tones of the mountains to match. Sometimes I still didn't believe I lived in this gorgeous place. I took a deep breath, stretched out my arms to my sides and wiggled my toes, working out the kinks.

The next mindless household chore awaited, actually something to which I looked forward after hours of mental concentration. When I was about halfway up the sidewalk alongside the garage, I stopped. There was something in the space the recycle barrel had occupied moments ago. About the size of a dinner plate, it was mottled tan and black. I moved only a hesitant step or two closer to confirm my suspicion: a coiled rattlesnake had been hiding beneath the raised bottom of the barrel. Probably fairly young, it wasn't moving or rattling.

Ken wasn't home. I was alone. There was no other way back into the house; the other doors were all locked. Even to call anyone, I'd have to edge, bare-toed, past the rattler to reach a phone inside.

I've held non-poisonous snakes several times—they're sleek and muscular, cool and dry to the touch—and even felt a little smug about feeling no fear. But today was different. I had no experience with potentially deadly snakes. Where I grew up, you could walk barefoot across your yard pretty confident you wouldn't be bitten by something that could kill you. I didn't know if this snake could kill me, but I knew it could cause great harm. It was small, but maybe it was more dangerous because it was small; I'd heard that's true of the scorpions here. My bare toes had been inches from the snake when I moved its hiding place—why didn't it strike?

Every spring and summer in Tucson, when the rattlers emerge from their winter hibernation, stories about their bites make the news. A few years before, a tiny girl walking with her mom was bitten by a snake hidden from her sight until it struck; she nearly died. A shopper in the garden department at a Tucson Wal-Mart was bitten by a three-and-half-foot rattler hiding behind bags of garden rock. A university instructor, wearing sandals, was walking through his neighborhood one evening when a huge rattler—later estimated as big around as his forearm—struck his foot. The venom, a highly toxic digestive juice, caused agonizing pain, intense swelling up to his rib cage, and permanent damage to his foot and lungs. An ensuing systemic infection from one of the punctures put him in the ICU a second time, for twice as long as his original stay.

In an instant, these stories flashed through my mind, more as sensation than words, yanked from memory by the startling appearance of the snake. Then another thought blossomed: The rattler could attack Ken, who had already come close to dying from two accidents in the previous five years. When he broke most of his ribs, which partially collapsed both lungs, the doctor said injuries like those frequently carry "significant mortality." As terrible as that was, it was a picnic compared to the hit-and-run that left him with a severe traumatic brain injury and weeks in rehab with more months of recovery after that. He still struggled at times to be who he used to be, to do what he so easily used to do.

I had been powerless to keep my husband safe out in the dangerous world where accidents happen and devastation blasted through the door of our cozy life without warning. I was helpless for months as he fought to survive and then to become whole again, or as whole as his injured brain would allow. Looking at that deadly, beautiful snake, the same fierce protectiveness welled up in me, the same as when I saw Ken delirious and thrashing in the ICU with a ventilator down his throat.

I would *not* let him be injured by this snake. What if it remained around our house (I'd heard they remained close to their home ground) and grew bigger, more venomous, then struck Ken or me when our attention wandered as we walked through the yard? I'd left the door open when I moved the barrels to the curb, so the rattler also had an opportunity to slither unnoticed into the garage and hide among the boxes and exercise equipment.

Probably no more than a minute or two passed as rushing adrenaline dredged up these memories and fears. Our neighbor was outside doing yard work, and he had dealt with rattlers on his property, so I walked out to the front of the house.

"Hey, Norm!" I waved, and he looked up. "Can you help me with something?"

He walked over, a cheerful gardener with bamboo rake in hand.

"I think there's a rattlesnake back here," I explained. "Ken's not home, and I don't know what to do."

We walked around to the side door. The snake, its elegant head centered within the coil, hadn't moved. Remaining at a safe distance, Norm nudged it a few times with his rake, and it wiggled. "Yeah, that's a rattler," he said. "See the rattles?"

"Yes." I saw two or three small ones.

"What do you want me to do with it?"

I didn't know. I hated the thought of killing it, yet mental images of fangs sinking into flesh, Ken's or mine, made my breath catch in my throat. "Should I call someone?" I asked. The fire department will send a crew to remove rattlers to another location, even though this snake didn't seem fearsome enough to warrant such a grandiose response.

"Nah," said Norm. "Should I just take it out into the desert, at the back of your lot?" The houses in our neighborhood stood on one-acre lots, a good portion of which remained untouched desert.

Norm once again used his rake to gently prod the snake and scoop it up. It was less than two feet long, graceful and sinuous across the splayed, bamboo teeth of the rake. Carefully, Norm carried it away from the house to more open ground in the side yard.

The snake was gorgeous. It was a living thing. It hadn't hurt anyone. But it could. It could grow up to be three or four feet long, and much more dangerous. It didn't mean us any harm; snakes had existed in the Sonoran Desert long before we did, and if it ever bit a human, it would only be following its nature, or what I, with my hazy understanding of snake behavior, believed to be its nature. But I didn't want it to exercise its natural impulses anywhere near me or Ken.

I fidgeted, trying to decide what to do. I trailed behind Norm, watching where I put my feet on the ground, which was splotched with bunches of dried brush and good-sized rocks— good camouflage for snakes.

"I guess we should kill it," I said. "Oh, I don't know. We could drop a big rock on it." Meaning, Norm could drop a big rock on it. "I don't know."

"I hate to kill a living thing," said Norm. "I could put him farther out and warn him not to come back. That might sound strange…"

It didn't sound all that strange to me. I'd read about people telling wild animals to stay away from their homes, which had worked. Still, this was a poisonous snake, and those other people were just trying to keep deer and raccoons from their garden.

"Won't it come back towards the house later?" I asked.

My sandaled feet felt exposed and vulnerable. I'd now always be nervous walking outside around the house, and maybe even inside. The possibility of a snake in our yard always existed; in fact, there were certainly others out there now.

"It could come back, sure," said Norm.

"How about a rock? Could you kill it with a rock?" A cruel death, but suitable rocks were all over the ground, and I couldn't think of another way. What should I do?

Agitation sent me into a strange dance, bouncing from foot to foot, with my hand to my mouth, then through my hair, then both arms wrapped around my middle. Not until later did I realize I had felt this same way when Ken's brain was newly broken and I could find no solid footing in that new reality. Again, confronted with the snake, welling anxiety clenched my chest and forced my blood to pound so hard I could hear it deep in my ears.

Norm waited for my decision.

Ken would have taken the snake out back into the desert. But he wasn't here. My chest ached as I decided. I was not making this decision in the same way I would choose what to have for dinner or where to go on vacation. I simply wanted to end the twitchy anxiety I would feel if the snake were still alive only yards from our home.

"Would you kill it?" I asked.

Norm hesitated. I knew he didn't want to do this. He's a kind, friendly man, very neighborly. And now a scared neighbor was asking him to smash a snake because she was afraid of what it might do to her or her husband in the future.

He picked up a hefty rock about the size of a large brick. As he dropped it, I turned away and cringed at the dull *thump*. But Norm couldn't get too close for fear of being bitten, so the rock didn't fall squarely on its target. On my behalf, he was torturing a living creature.

"No. This won't work," said Norm.

I squirmed, hating to be the cause of such pain, for both the snake and Norm. But now that the snake was injured, we had to finish the job. Finish the killing.

"Do you have a shovel?" asked Norm.

In the garage, I took a heavy shovel from the wall rack

where we stored yard implements and carried it out to Norm. Three or four times he jammed the straight edge down across the snake, producing a metallic clang against the hard desert earth, finally severing the head, which he buried under some sand and a rock.

He held out the bloodied body towards me, rattles at the top. "Do you think Ken would like to see it?"

I focused my eyes near the small rattles, away from the ragged decapitation site, and also tried to not to look too closely at the several gashes on the dorsal side. The tan underside, smooth and unblemished, reminded me of suede. I reached to grasp the body near the rattles. It felt weirdly mushy between my fingers; startled, I jerked my hand back. I reached for it again and held it between my thumb and forefinger, my arm out-stretched. The ropelike body curled slightly once or twice, then went limp.

Ken gets woozy at the sight of blood. He wouldn't want to see it.

I carried the lifeless, mangled snake to the trash barrel, lifted the lid, and tossed it in. It fell on the kitchen trash bag I'd carried out only a few minutes before, its earth-colored markings a clear contrast to the white plastic. Later, I wondered why I hadn't asked Norm also to bury the body, to show at least some respect to this living creature whose execution I had ordered.

Norm and I looked at each other. "Thanks," I said, looking uneasily into his eyes. Sadness, and maybe defeat, radiated from him. What did he think of me? "I'm sorry about all this."

"It's okay," he replied quietly and headed back to his house.

I turned to look at the trash barrel. "I'm sorry."

Walking back to the side door and into the garage, I put away the shovel with a quivering hand. My whole body ached, as if I was coming down with the flu. Already, now that the danger had been dispatched, and in such an awful way, I was thinking I'd overreacted.

When I told Ken about the snake later that evening, he was disappointed in me and a little angry. "I would have carried it out into the desert," he said. I knew that but had hoped for more understanding from him. My emotions flared, but I was too exhausted and confused to say much. By the time we went to bed, though, Ken's anger had cooled and he said he understood my asking Norm to kill the snake.

That night, I dreamt of a hulking, hairy monster in the distance, walking away from me and trailing an ominous feeling. Was I the monster?

In a perfect bit of synchronicity, I'd recently read an article about surveys in which people typically characterize themselves as kind and patient, but then, out in the world, they yell at grocery store checkers when the wait is too long, or pound on their car horns and give the finger to old people who drive too slowly. I had thought of myself as gentle and peace-loving, except for the occasional insect-stomping. Now, though, I had not only committed the most violent act in which I'd ever been involved, but also implored someone else to do the dirty work. At first I hedged when telling the story, saying vaguely, "We decided it was best to kill it," without fully revealing how "we" accomplished it. Only after several days could I admit outright to pushing Norm to kill the snake and hesitantly explain the ugly method of execution, accepting as my punishment the horrified or angry responses of most listeners.

A little belated research revealed facts about rattlesnakes that, had I known them in advance, might have helped me make a more rational decision when confronted by one. With the air so cool and the hour too early for normal hunting time, the snake might well have let me pass into the garage (although the thought of walking bare-toed just inches away was unnerving). It had not rattled and did not move at all until Norm gently nudged it with his rake, and then only barely. If Ken had been home, if another door had been unlocked, if I had accepted Norm's offer to move the snake away from the house, we would not have killed it. Without having read those accounts of rattler bites and the damage they could inflict, or having seen Ken suffer so much after his accidents and endured the agony with him, would I still have wanted that snake dead?

It really didn't matter. Knowing I had such a capacity for cruelty unsettled me deeply. The snake was part of Perfect Love, but I had failed miserably in remembering that. All I could do now was remain contrite about my responsibility for the brutal killing of a sentient being that had not harmed me.

After a few days, I stopped talking about it and did my best to put away the whole disturbing episode in memory.

Months later, I looked up at the high shelf in our kitchen and noticed how everything needed a good dusting. The silk flower arrangement, the blue and yellow Oaxacan tiger carving, the quirky wooden crane, even the edge of the shelf were sporting fuzzy edges. Alongside them, a toy snake in a Nepalese bowl caught my attention as it hadn't in a very long time. It had been a dozen years since Snake in its golden vessel first visited me during a spirituality workshop I'd attended.

Indiana, Spring 1995

It figured I'd be the only one to raise my hand. Nigel, the workshop leader, had asked if anyone present was wrestling with a dilemma. Certainly everyone must be, I thought, and then watched in dismay as no other hands went up.

"Barbara, come up here and let's see if we can't help you

figure out how to resolve your dilemma," Nigel beckoned in his Australian accent that charmed my Midwestern ears.

Feeling like a game-show contestant, I walked down the aisle between the rows of chairs set up in the Indianapolis hotel banquet room and approached the low platform. Nigel had been taking us through a weekend workshop called "The Awakening," where we could "pursue the ultimate truth to the questions surrounding our current existence." He asked me to sit on the tall chair there, and I did, facing the rest of the group while wondering what I'd gotten myself into.

Nigel did not ask me to reveal my dilemma, only to imagine it having two sides. That wasn't hard. Only fifteen months earlier, I had liberated myself from that well-paid but emotionally stifling corporate PR job to become a freelance writer. Being 42 at the time, I joked about my mid-life crisis, but my hope was to discover and follow the creative yearnings of my heart while supporting myself through them.

I silently named the two sides of my dilemma Creativity and Support.

"I'm all set," I said. "What's next?"

"Hold your hands out in front of you, palms up, and visualize those two sides of your dilemma taking on physical form, one in each hand," he explained. "Then ask them to work together to find a solution."

I was game. I'd done enough visualization to be comfortable with it, even in front of several dozen people. Nigel was asking me to use my imagination to "see" my dilemma in whatever way my subconscious offered up, which could direct me to a creative way of dealing with it on a level much deeper than any literal or "rational" method. So I settled back in the chair, propped my feet on the bar between its front legs, and, receptive, held my palms up and open to the air. The audience disappeared behind my closed eyelids, and I felt myself relaxing and then expanding inward into my consciousness.

Within a few seconds, a friendly reptile, coiled and green, appeared on my upturned right hand and stared through his ebony eyes into my mind's eye, as if to say, "Here I am. Now what are you going to do with me?"

How perfect! I thought. Snake is an ancient symbol for many things, including creativity, transformation, and fertility of imagination. This was a cool exercise!

Next, a form appeared in my left palm. It resembled a chunk of golden clay, lustrous and mysterious. It did not speak or otherwise communicate with me or Snake. I couldn't figure out what it might represent.

I sat for a few more minutes, enjoying my vision and waiting to see if the chunk would do anything. But nothing more happened. Trusting that my subconscious knew what it was doing, I decided more of this vision would eventually be revealed. I opened my eyes and explained to Nigel and my fellow seekers what had happened and then walked back to my chair in the audience.

The day after returning home, I read about Snake in my Medicine Card packet, which I was then using as a meditation aid by asking a question and then pulling a card from the shuffled deck. Some people believe that the subconscious chooses the card we most need to see at the moment. Whether that was true or not, I was ready to find meaning or a new perspective in whatever card I chose, just as I had with the figures of Snake and the chunk during the workshop. The explanation of the Snake card read, in part, "If you have chosen this symbol, there is a need within you to transmute some thought, action, or desire so that wholeness may be achieved. This is heavy magic, but remember, magic is no more than a change in consciousness."

Magic is no more than a change in consciousness.

A change in consciousness meant changing my thoughts about something, about how I perceive it or react to it. And if that shift helped me to feel better or solve a problem—or even revealed there was no real problem at all—then that was the magic.

I sat down on my couch to do the visualization again. Eyes closed, palms upward, I asked that more of the message be revealed. My palms grew warm, and both forms reappeared, Snake on the right, chunk on the left. Suddenly, with no conscious thought on my part, the chunk began spinning as if on a potter's wheel, fashioning itself into a vessel of some sort, a tall vase or a chalice. Its golden sides grew tall and burnished. The mouth flared out, receptive and open. When it was complete, Snake crawled over and coiled inside. It raised its sleek head over the edge and peered at me again.

The image faded and the heat in my palms cooled.

Now what? The amazing image obviously held great significance, but what was it? There was the sexual imagery, which could be interpreted in various ways—fertility or creativity, for example. Perhaps the vessel represented my own consciousness, which would gestate and give birth to my creativity, in writing and other ways.

Fine, I thought. That's interesting.

But why hadn't Snake spoken profound words? Why hadn't a life-altering message from the universe been written on the side of the vessel? Why did I have to figure this out myself? I needed something clear and dramatic. Some big message from the Universe that would blast me to The Path I Was Supposed To Follow. This was not like Saul's lightning bolt on the way to Damascus; this was more like the puny flickering of a match. I was sorely disappointed.

After a few more minutes of sitting there puzzled and frustrated, I gave up trying to interpret the symbolism. But I honored my vision by finding a way to transform it from imagination into 3-D reality: When I later bought a flat-bottomed Nepalese bowl of hammered copper—not a chalice, but it would do—I placed in it a card my friend Teresa had sent after I told her of my vision. The card was cut in the shape of a slithering rattlesnake. Later, after moving to Tucson, I found a rattlesnake stuffed animal, coiled and tan, arranged it in the bowl with its head hanging over the side, then placed the bowl on the high kitchen shelf with other decorative items. I saw it there often, a cute reminder of my vision as well as a playful nod to my new home in the desert.

Tucson, Winter 2007

On the day I noticed the dust, it was as if Snake again came to life and wriggled down off the shelf, roused by all the commotion over the dead rattlesnake. It reminded me of my Medicine Cards, which I hadn't used very much in years and so hadn't thought to consult after the killing. They were tucked in a basket next to the fireplace, along with boxes of various other divination cards, serving now more as decoration than meditation tool. I flipped through the book that explained the Medicine Cards to the page about Snake and again read: "If you have chosen this symbol, there is a need within you to transmute some thought, action, or desire so that wholeness may be achieved. This is heavy magic, but remember, magic is no more than a change in consciousness."

That phrase again: *magic is no more than a change in consciousness.* I remembered it now, and it comforted me. This time, the symbol chosen hadn't been a piece of decorated cardboard or a product of my imagination but a live animal I had brutally slaughtered. Perhaps by interpreting this symbol for myself, I could finally use its magic to understand the reason for my terrible act.

So I sat in my favorite wing chair, relaxed and with eyes closed. My breath slowed, and instead of holding my palms upward as before, I kept my hands in my lap and simply held Snake in my mind, asking silently for an answer. Instead of pushing aside my sadness over the killing of the rattlesnake, as I had been doing, I let it rise up and open my heart.

Slowly, a memory emerged, and I rode along to see where it would take me.

One evening sometime before the brain wreck, Ken discovered a young rattlesnake on the patio, stretched out full-length in the gap between the sections of concrete. I saw it, too, through a window. Ken even took a photo of it before nudging it out into the yard with a long stick. It may have returned, but we never saw it again. That time, having a poisonous snake so close to our house was more a goose-bumpy thrill of living in the desert than a reason for all-out panic.

That time, Ken had been home. That time, the snake had not startled me as I realized my bare toes had come within inches of it. Neither had I yet read so many accounts of rattlesnake bites and the damage they can do, nor endured the post-accident terror of Ken's brain wreck.

Wait. The brain wreck. Here was the answer. When Ken came home after that accident, I had to release my fear that he would somehow be hurt again in spite of my care. When he wanted to return to work so soon, I had to release my fear of his being out in the world where I could not protect him. With time, I had done both of these things, and also thought myself healed.

But now, even four years later, it was clear that another hidden pool of fear remained—but not about Ken. As much as I did not want him to suffer so terribly any more, I feared even more having to endure my own version of that torture along with him. The torture of a wife who didn't know if her husband would come home again. Who didn't know if her husband's injured brain would ever allow him to read or work or be the same intelligent, self-aware man with whom she'd fallen in love and married. Who didn't know how long she could continue to care for him more like a mother or a nurse than as a wife. Who feared more than anything that the brain injury, which had kidnapped him, might also have replaced him with a stranger she could not love, and no amount of ransom she could ever hope to pay would bring back her precious Ken.

True, none of these fears had come to pass. But all those nights when Ken was hospitalized and I could not sleep, and all those days when he forgot my name and smiled vacantly and was not present even though he sat next to me, they hissed and snarled in my ear. Then they whispered in my head long after his homecoming. I had never voiced them, and could barely stand to think them; they were disloyal and too weighted with sorrow. However, in order to function, I had shoved them deep underground, where they became a smoldering seam of coal layered beneath the earth, ready to flash without warning. I thought them long extinguished, but they exploded that day last spring, and the poor snake had been both spark and victim.

Now I understood.

And then came the insight by which I could transmute my sadness into understanding and begin to feel whole again: I had endured my own anguish over Ken's accident, yet had never fully acknowledged how much I had suffered, too. During Ken's recovery, a counselor told me that most likely I had been affected by secondary traumatic stress, which can befall a caregiver whose loved one is the primary victim of a horrible trauma. I'd forgotten about this conversation until now, and could see its truth.

The rattlesnake at the side of the house instantly and unconsciously became the symbol for the awful events through which my husband and I had lived. By frightening me, it ripped open the thin membrane in which I'd wrapped those memories, allowing my old protective feelings towards Ken to flood out through the gap. So I acted, however irrationally, to remove the threat.

I will always feel remorse for killing the snake, but because it came to me that day, I was able to own up to those old snarling fears, release them, and regain wholeness—or at least begin the process. My thanks to the snake is both penance and blessing: I'll remember my role in its sacrifice so that when overpowering fear threatens me again (how can one live without such times?), I will not bury it. Instead, I will drag it out into the light, look it in the eye, and face it as honestly as I can.

Printed in the United States
203425BV00002B/151-177/P